Paradigms for Fast Parallel Approximability

**Cambridge International Series
on Parallel Computation**

Managing Editor:

W.F. McColl, *Programming Research Group, University of Oxford*

Editorial Board:

T.F. Chan, *Department of Mathematics, University of California at Los Angeles*
A. Gottlieb, *Courant Institute, New York University*
R.M. Karp, *Computer Science Division, University of California at Berkeley*
M. Rem, *Department of Mathematics and Computer Science, Eindhoven University of Technology*
L.G. Valiant, *Aiken Computation Laboratory, Harvard University*

Cambridge International Series in Parallel Computation: 8

PARADIGMS FOR FAST PARALLEL APPROXIMABILITY

Josep Díaz
Maria Serna
Paul Spirakis
Jacobo Torán

CAMBRIDGE
UNIVERSITY PRESS

CAMBRIDGE UNIVERSITY PRESS
Cambridge, New York, Melbourne, Madrid, Cape Town, Singapore, São Paulo, Delhi

Cambridge University Press
The Edinburgh Building, Cambridge CB2 8RU, UK

Published in the United States of America by Cambridge University Press, New York

www.cambridge.org
Information on this title: www.cambridge.org/9780521117920

First published 1997
This digitally printed version 2009

A catalogue record for this publication is available from the British Library

Library of Congress Cataloguing in Publication data

Paradigms for fast parallel approximability / Josep Díaz ... [et al.].
p.   cm. – (Cambridge International series on parallel computation ; 8)
Includes bibliographical references and index.
ISBN 0 521 43170 0 (hc)
1. Parallel processing (Electronic computers)   I. Díaz, J. (Josep), 1950–   .   II. Series.
QA76.58.P3355   1997
511'.6'0285435–dc21   96-51778   CIP

ISBN 978-0-521-43170-5 hardback
ISBN 978-0-521-11792-0 paperback

Contents

Preface

This monograph surveys the recent developments in the field of parallel approximability to combinatorial optimization problems. The book is designed not specifically as a textbook, but as a sedimentation of a great deal of research done on this specific topic. Accordingly, we do not include a collection of exercises, but throughout the text we comment about different open research problems in the field. The monograph can easily be used as a support for advanced courses in either parallel or sequential algorithms, or for a graduate course on the topic.

In Chapter 1, we motivate the topic of parallel approximability, using an example. In the same chapter we keep the reasoning at a very intuitive level, and we survey some of the techniques and concepts that will be assumed throughout the book, like randomization and derandomization. In Chapter 2 we give a formal presentation of algorithms for the Parallel Random Access Machines model. We survey some of the known results on sequential approximability, and introduce the basic definitions and classes used in the theory of Parallel Approximability. The core of the book, Chapters 3 to 7, forms a collection of *paradigms* to produce parallel approximations. The word "paradigm" has a different semantic from the one used by Kuhn, in the sense that we use paradigm as a particular property or technique that can be used to give approximations in parallel for a whole class of problems. Chapter 3 presents the use of *extremal graph theory*, to obtain approximability to some graph problems. Chapter 4 presents parallel approximability results for profit/cost problems using the *rounding, interval partitioning* and *separation* techniques. Full parallel approximation schemes are presented for the Subset Sum problem, and several problems on flows and matchings. Chapter 5 presents the paradigm of *primal–dual* and its application to obtain parallel approximation schemes to problems that can be solved using positive linear programming. In Chapter 6 we take advantage of the *graph decomposition* of planar graphs into k-outerplanar graphs, to obtain parallel approximation schemes for a series of graph problems, when the input is restricted to planar graphs. There is not a clear underlying paradigm in Chapter 7. The contents of that chapter are problems for which their parallel approximability follows (non-trivially) from the sequential approximability. In particular we consider parallel approximation to the Traveling Salesperson problem and the Bin Packing problem. Chapter 8 presents some parallel non-approximability results, in the sense that the approximation problems considered are P-hard. We are aware that P-hardness is not the ultimate indicator for the non-existence of a parallel solution, but as we have been considering the PRAM model of massive parallel computation, the P-hardness of a problem indicates the difficulty of obtaining an efficient (NC) solution to the problem. The chapter complements results given in Chapters 4, 5 and 7. Finally the last chapter of the book is devoted to syntactically defined approximability classes and the behavior of problems in these classes with respect to parallel approximability. The book ends with the formal definition, in an appendix, of the problems introduced through the text.

We assume that the reader has a certain maturity in the field of sequential and parallel algorithms. Basic techniques in design of PRAM algorithms are not given. Other than that the book is self-contained. Although we present the basic definitions and facts of sequential approximability, it is not the purpose of the book to study the topic of sequential approximation, and we point the interested reader to the references at the beginning of Chapter 2.

The genesis of the monograph, was a number of expository talks given by some of the authors on *Paradigms for NC Approximations*, WOPA 1994, Daghstul Seminar on Probabilistic Methods 1994, DIMACS workshop 1994, and an invited lecture at LATIN-95.

Several people have read previous versions of the manuscript and made valuable comments: Ricard Gavaldà, Ray Greenlaw, Jozef Gruska, Luca Trevisan, Vijai Vazirani and Fatos Xhafa. Thanks to them the quality of the manuscript was improved. We also would like to thank the anonymous referees and D. Tranah for their efforts in improving the readability of the manuscript.

The work done in this book was financed by Project 20244 of the European Commission (ALCOM-IT).

1

Introduction

In this chapter we provide an intuitive introduction to the topic of approximability and parallel computation. The method of approximation is one of the well established ways of coping with computationally hard optimization problems. Many important problems are known to be NP-hard, therefore assuming the plausible hypothesis that P$\neq$NP, it would be impossible to obtain polynomial time algorithms to solve these problems.

In Chapter 2, we will give a formal definition of optimization problem, and a formal introduction to the topics of PRAM computation and approximability. For the purpose of this chapter, in an optimization problem the goal is to find a solution that maximizes or minimizes an objective function subjected to some constrains. Let us recall that in general to study the NP-completeness of an optimization problem, we consider its decision version. The decision version of many optimization problems is NP-complete, while the optimization version is NP-hard (see for example the book by Garey and Johnson [GJ79]). To refresh the above concepts, let us consider the Maximum Cut problem (MAXCUT).

Given a graph G with a set V of n vertices and a set E of edges, the MAXCUT problem asks for a partition of V into two disjoint sets V_1 and V_2 that maximizes the number of edges crossing between V_1 and V_2. From now on through all the manuscript, all graphs have a finite number of vertices n. The foregoing statement of the MAXCUT problem is the optimization version and it is known to be NP-hard [GJ79]. The decision version of MAXCUT has as instance a graph $G = (V, E)$ and a bound $k \in \mathbb{Z}^+$, and the problem is to find the partition V_1 and V_2 such that the number of edges crossing the two sets of vertices is greater than or equal to k. The decision version of MAXCUT is NP-complete [GJS76]. The MAXCUT is a problem of great practical importance in the design of interconnexion networks and in statistical physics (see for example [BGJR88]).

Decision problems are easy to encode as languages over a finite alphabet, where for each problem the language is the set of instances having answer *yes*. Given an instance of a decision problem, to test if it has a solution is equivalent to deciding if the instance belongs to the language. The theory of NP-completeness was developed at the beginning of the 70s, in terms of decision problems ([Coo71], [Lev73], [Kar72]). The idea of approximate difficult problems is previous to the development of the theory of NP-completeness [Gra66]. Johnson in a seminal paper [Joh74] did a systematic treatment to approximate in polynomial time the solution to many of the optimization versions in the original list of NP-complete problems, given by Karp [Kar72]. Since then, the topic has become a standard part in courses on algorithms (see for example [CLR89]). Intuitively, for $0 < \epsilon \leq 1$, an ϵ-**approximation** is an algorithm that outputs a value s, such that the optimal solution lies in the interval $[s\epsilon, s/\epsilon]$.

Concurrently with this development of approximability to hard problems, in order to gain speed and computer power, research in parallel architectures was flourishing. As a consequence, a lot of work was taking place developing the foundations of massive parallel computation and parallel algorithm design. The most popular theoretical model of parallel computation that has been used is the **Parallel Random Access Machine** (PRAM), introduced by Fortune and Wyllie [FW78] and by Goldschlager [Gol78]. A PRAM consists of a number of sequential RAM processors, each with its own memory, working synchronously and communicating among themselves through a common shared memory. In one step, each processor can access one memory location (for reading or writting on it), or execute a single RAM operation. Although performing the same instructions, the processors can act on different data.

The simplicity of the PRAM model has led to its acceptance as the model used to identify the structural characteristics that allow us to exploit parallelism for solving the problem. However, it should be noted that the PRAM model hides levels of algorithmic and programming complexity concerning *reliability, synchronization, data locality* and *message passing*. Nevertheless, as we shall mention in Section 1.3, several techniques have been developed to simulate PRAM algorithms by more realistic models of parallel computation.

1.1 Sequential and Parallel Computation

The sequential model we use is the RAM machine, in which we measure **time** by number of steps and **space** by number of memory locations. As usual by an **efficient** sequential algorithm we mean one that takes polynomial time using a RAM machine. The set of problems that can be solved by such algorithms constitute the class **P**. To familiarize the reader with the notation we use to describe algorithms, let us give a program for the Prefix-Sums problem. The input to the Prefix-Sums problem is a sequence $(x_1, \ldots, x_n)$, and the output is a sequence $(s_1, \ldots, s_n)$ where for each $1 \leq i \leq n$, $s_i = \sum_{j=1}^{i} x_j$. In Algorithm 1 we give the sequential code for the Prefix-Sums operation.

PRESUMS $(x[1:n])$

1    $s[1] := x[1];$

2   **for** $i = 2$ **to** n **do**

3       $s[i] := s[i-1] + x[i]$

Algorithm 1: Sequential Prefix-Sums

The use of a parallel machine changes the parameters to measure efficiency. In sequential RAM models, the usual measure is time, and to a lesser extent space. In the parallel setting we have to measure the use of two resources, number of parallel steps (parallel time) and the maximum number of processors needed in any parallel step. By an **efficient** parallel algorithm we mean one that takes polylogarithmic time using a polynomial number of processors, and can be implemented on a PRAM machine. Problems that can be solved within these constraints are said to belong to the class **NC**. Thus problems in class NC are regarded as being solved in parallel, using a polylogarithmic number of parallel steps and using a number of processors that at most is polynomial, both measure functions in the size of the input to the problem. Through all this book, given a problem, we shall refer to an NC *algorithm* as a parallel algorithm for the problem that can be implemented with a PRAM using a polylogarithmic number of steps and a polynomial number of processors. The same abuse of nomenclature will be used with other parallel complexity classes, like RNC and ZNC.

We write parallel algorithms in an informal pseudolanguage. The description of an algorithm is given in sequences of macroinstructions. The main difference from sequential algorithms is the use of a new instruction **for all** ⟨condition⟩ **pardo**; all statements following this sentence are executed in parallel for all processors whose identifier satisfies the condition. Algorithm 2 solves the Prefix-Sums problem in a PRAM, for sake of simplicity we have assumed that the input data is indexed from 0 to $n-1$.

PPRESUMS $(x[0:n-1])$

1   **for** $d = 1$ **to** $\log n$ **do**

2   **for all** $i \bmod 2^{d+1} = 0$ and $0 \leq i \leq n$ **pardo**

3           $x[i + 2^{d+1} - 1] := x[i + 2^d - 1] + x[i + 2^{d+1} - 1]$

Algorithm 2: Parallel Prefix-Sums

In general we will use the product time × processors to derive bounds that allow us to compare the performance of sequential and parallel algorithms. Notice that a parallel step involving n processors can be performed by a single processor in time n. The above algorithm takes time $O(\log n)$ and uses $O(n)$ processors. Thus if we use a sequential machine to simulate the algorithm the simulation will take time $O(n \log n)$; therefore the parallel algorithm is not optimal.

An optimal parallel algorithm will be one such that the product × processors is equal to the optimal (best bound) sequential complexity. It is relatively easy to derive an optimal implementation of the above algorithm (see for example [JaJ92], [Rei93]), although we will not give it here. The Prefix-Sums operation has been analyzed for centuries as the recurrence $x_i = a_1 + x_{i-1}$. The first parallel circuit was suggested by Ofman [Ofm63].

1.2 Some Problems to Approximate

Let us begin with an easy example of a problem that can be approximated in parallel. The Maximum Satisfiability problem consists in, given a boolean formula F in conjunctive normal form, finding a truth assignment that satisfies the maximum number of clauses simultaneosuly. It is easy to derive an approximation algorithm for the Maximum Satisfiability problem. Note that the assignment $x_i = 1$ (for $1 \leq i \leq n$) satisfies all clauses with a positive literal and the assignment $x_i = 0$ (for $1 \leq i \leq n$) satisfies all the clauses with a negative literal. Therefore, given a boolean formula F with m clauses and with variables $x_1, \ldots, x_n$, taking from the two previous assignments the one satisfying most clauses, such an assignment satisfies at least $m/2$ clauses, and since there are m clauses, it is at least "half as good" as an optimal assignment. Also it is easy to see that with a polynomial number of processors it can be checked in logarithmic time whether an assignment satisfies at least one half of the clauses, and therefore this provides a trivial parallel algorithm for approximating Maximum Satisfiability within a constant factor of the optimal solution.

Let us move to a more involved example, the Maximum Cut problem. In the following, we shall prove that there is a PRAM algorithm to approximate MAXCUT within a constant factor of the optimal solution. The proof uses the technique of *derandomization*. Our presentation is based on the paper by Luby [Lub86].

To clarify the proof, let us consider the 0-1 Labeling problem. Given a graph $G = (V, E)$, with n nodes, a **labeling** is an assignment of labels from the set $\{0, 1\}$ to the nodes of G. For a labeling $l : V \to \{0, 1\}$ define the **cost** of the labeling l by $X(l) = \sum_{\{u,v\} \in E} |l(u) - l(v)|$. The 0-1 Labeling problem consists in finding the labeling that maximizes the cost. Thus taking as partition the set of vertices with the same label the labeling problem is equivalent to the MAXCUT problem.

Notice that for a graph with n vertices, there are 2^n possible labelings of it. A naive aproach to solving the problem is a search in the whole space of labelings, as is done in Algorithm 3. Notice that we can represent a labeling by a binary string x taking values from 0^n to 1^n. The variable c computes the maximum cost of all labelings, so at the end the value of c will be the maximal cost, and the variable l will hold a labeling with maximal cost.

MAXCUT (G)

```
1   n := |V|; c := 0; l := 2^n;
2   for x = 0 to 2^n − 1 do
3       d := 0;
4       for i = 1 to n do
5           for j = i + 1 to n do
6               if (i, j) ∈ E and x_i ≠ x_j
7                   then d := d + 1;
8       if d > c then
9           c := d; l := x
```

Algorithm 3: Solving MAXCUT by exhaustive search

Although Algorithm 3 takes exponential time, we can investigate further properties of the cost function. Given G, let Ω denote the set of all 2^n possible labelings. We can see the set Ω as a probability space, in which each labeling is a sample point, to be taken with probability $1/|\Omega|$, and the function X is interpreted as a random variable on Ω. Therefore one can ask about the average cost of a labeling. The expected value of X, denoted by $\mu[X]$, is defined as

$$\mu[X] = \sum_{l \in \Omega} X(l) \Pr\{l\}.$$

To find a bound for the expectation, let us consider an alternative scheme. For each node $u \in V$ define an indicator random variable l_u that takes values 0 and 1 with probability $1/2$. Consider n independent random variables, one for each node $u \in V$. Notice that the *joint distribution* of the n independent random variables is the uniform distribution on the set Ω. Therefore we can express the expectation through labelings or through the outcome of the n random variables. The main difference is that now we have only to analyze the contribution of each edge to the final cost. A given edge contributes 0 when both labels are the same, but when they differ the contribution is 1. Therefore we can express the expectation as

$$\mu[X] = \sum_{e=(u,v) \in E} (1 \Pr\{l_u = l_v\} + 0 \Pr\{l_u \neq l_v\}). \tag{1.1}$$

Recall that l_u is selected from $\{0, 1\}$, with probability $1/2$, and as the random variables are independent, we get

$$\Pr\{l_u = l_v\} = \Pr\{l_u = 1 \text{ and } l_v = 1\} + \Pr\{l_u = 0 \text{ and } l_v = 0\}$$
$$= \frac{1}{4} + \frac{1}{4} = \frac{1}{2},$$

and also we obtain the same value for the probability of being different. Thus, substituting in (1.1) we conclude that

$$\mu[X] = \sum_{e=(u,v) \in E} \frac{1}{2} = \frac{|E|}{2}.$$

This probabilistic result says that if an element of Ω is generated at random, then with high probability (greater than or equal to $1/2$) we will have an element for which the cost function is greater than or equal to the expected value. In Algorithm 4 we present a simple schema that with high probability computes a labeling with a cost above the average.

This algorithm can be easily parallelized, just replace the sequential **for**

RCUT (G)
1   $n := |V|$;
2   **for** $i = 1$ **to** n **do**
3   toss a fair coin to assign a value 0 or 1 to $l[i]$

Algorithm 4: Computing with high probability a cut at least average

---

PRCUT (G)
1   $n := |V|$;
2   **for all** $1 \leq i \leq n$ **pardo**
3   toss a fair coin to assign a value 0 or 1 to $l[i]$

Algorithm 5: Computing with high probability a cut at least average in parallel

by a **forall** sentence, as is done in Algorithm 5. Thus we have a randomized parallel algorithm that in constant time, using n processors, with high probability produces a labeling with cost at least the average cost. It is not difficult to do a better analysis. The average cost is $|E|/2$ and the maximum cost is bounded above by the total number $|E|$ of edges in the graph. Thus if we could compute a value c' such that $|E|/2 \leq c' \leq |E|$ then we are sure that the optimum cost is in the interval $[c', 2\,c']$. Therefore, c' is a $\frac{1}{2}$-approximation to the optimal cut. Thus algorithms RCUT and PRCUT are randomized algorithms that with high probability produce a $\frac{1}{2}$-approximation to the optimal cut.

However, we want a deterministic algorithm; to get it, we use a general technique used to derandomize some algorithms. Nice introductions to derandomization techniques are given in Chapter 15 of the book of Alon, Spencer and Erdös [ASE92] and the Ph. Dissertation of Berger [Ber90]. The key observation is that in the expectation analysis we only make use of the fact that the labels of two elements are independent, and we did not need the independence of a larger set of labels. Therefore to have a probability space in which the analysis of the expectation is the same as before, we need a labeling space in which two properties hold: the first one, that the probability of a node getting label 0 (1) is 1/2; the second one, that the labels of any two elements must be independent. This last property is usually called **pairwise independence**. The interesting point in this approach is that while a probability space with full independence has exponential size, it is possible to construct a probability space of polynomial size, with only pairwise independence. Clearly, if a random variable over the small space takes a value with positive probability, then some element of the space must be bigger than or equal to this value. Therefore by exhaustive search the small space can be used to derive a non-random algorithm.

In our case, the main idea to get the polynomial space of labeling is to start with a set of polynomial size, in which an element can be described with few bits, and then use some kind of *hash function* to determine the corresponding labeling. The notion of hash function or hash table appears when we want to address a small number of elements, stored in a huge array. Here the small set represents the set of keys, assigned to labelings. Furthermore, consider hash funcions as random variables, over the set of keys, K, with uniform distribution.

To be precise, take the set of keys K as the set of pairs (a, b) with $1 \leq a, b \leq n$, so K has n^2 points. Define the labeling associated to key (a, b) in the following way:

$$l_{a,b}(v) = \begin{cases} 0 & \text{if } a + bv \text{ is even,} \\ 1 & \text{otherwise.} \end{cases}$$

Fix a vertex $v \in V$; considering all possible elements in K, the corresponding labeling assigns label 1 to v in one half of the cases, and 0 in the other half. But that means that in the space of labelings addressed through K the probability that v gets label 0 (1) is 1/2. Therefore the first requirement if fulfilled.

Now fix two vertices u and v, and consider all elements in $K \times K$. For a given tuple $(a, b, c, d) \in K \times K$ the corresponding labelings assign the same label to both vertices when $x = a + bu + c + dv$ is even, and different labels when x is odd. A straightforward computation gives that for half of the elements in $K \times K$ the corresponding x value will be even and for the other half it will be odd, therefore the probability that two labelings agree (or disagree) on two nodes is 1/2. Thus the analysis of $\mu[X]$ can be done, in the space of labelings obtained through K, and the new expected value is still bounded by $|E|$.

This property guarantees that if we search through all points in the small space and take the one with maximum cost, we get a labeling that has cost bigger than or equal to the average cost. Therefore, performing an exahustive search, we can obtain a $\frac{1}{2}$-approximation to the problem. The foregoing argument implies that Algorithm 6 computes an approximation to the MAXCUT on a given graph $G = (V, E)$. The labeling corresponding to the final values of $a1, b1$ is a $\frac{1}{2}$-approximation to the MAXCUT on G. Moreover, the complexity of the algorithm is $O(1)$ parallel steps and it uses $O(n^4)$ processors.

     MAXCUT (G)
1 $n := |V|; c := 0; a1 := 0; b1 := 0;$
2 **for all** $1 \leq a, b \leq n$ **pardo**
3   **for all** $1 \leq i, j \leq n$ **pardo**
4   **if** $(i, j) \in E$ and $a + bi + a + bj$ is odd
5   **then** $l[\langle a, b \rangle, \langle i, j \rangle] := 1;$
6   PPRESUMS$(l[\langle a, b \rangle]);$
7 **for** $d = 1$ **to** $2 \log n$ **do**
8   **for all** $i \bmod 2^{d+1}$ and $0 \leq i \leq n$ **pardo**
9        $l[i + 2^{d+1} - 1, 2n] :=$
             $\max(l[i + 2^d - 1, 2n], l[i + 2^{d+1} - 1, 2n]);$
10   $c := l[2n, 2n]/2$

Algorithm 6: Approximating MAXCUT in parallel.

Algorithm 6 illustrates one of the canonical techniques to obtain approximations with NC algorithms. In the following chapters, we will describe different techniques to approximate in parallel difficult problems. We will define different parallel approximation complexity classes, and study the consequences of a problem being in one of those classes, as well as the relationship among the classes.

1.3 Realistic Models

An important matter for the reader could be the use of the PRAM machine as our model of parallel computation. At the beginning of the chapter, we already indicated that the PRAM model provides a robust framework for the development and analysis of parallel algorithms, as it is a formal model to measure the amount of inherent parallelism in a given problem. Quite a bit of work has been done in studying whether a PRAM algorithm can be efficiently implemented on a "realistic" parallel machine, by realistic meaning

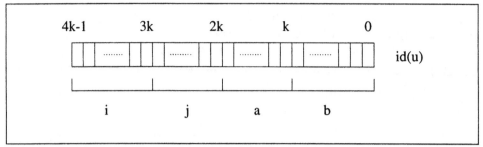

Fig. 1.1: Interpretation of the identifier of a node

a machine that takes into account factors such as the data locality, the synchronization or the cost of message passing. This last issue is one of the most relevant points in the simulation, and basically depends on the **bisection width** or **bandwidth** of the underlying topology connecting the processors in the realistic machine. The bandwidth is the maximum number of messages per instruction that can pass between one half of the processors and the other half. In general, while the PRAM model has unlimited bandwidth, most of the real machines have limited bandwidth, the exception being the hypercube (see for example the book of Leighton for a deep study of synchronous networks of processors [Lei93]). It should be noticed that there are efforts towards building machines with very high bandwidth, like the TERA machine [ACC90] and the PRAM being built at Saarbrücken [ADK⁺93].

In general a PRAM algorithm could be implemented on a distributed memory machine with not too much loss of efficiency, depending on the number of processors used and the size of the data. Most of the simulations will take a polylogarithmic cost in the number of parallel steps (see for example the survey papers by McColl [McC93] and Ranade [Ran96]).

Let us show how to implement the algorithm described for the Maximum Cut problem, on a real machine, the hypercube. A q-dimensional hypercube is formed by 2^q synchronous processors, each processor with a different identifier of q bits, a processor is connected to all processors at Hamming distance one. Processors may have the computing capacity we wish; from being workstations to processors with a few bits of memory.

Assume that $n = 2^k$ for some k, and consider a $4k$-dimensional hypercube, notice that now each node has an identifier formed by $4k$ bits. This identifier $id(u)$ will be divided into 4 numbers of k bits each (see Figure 1.1). The first $2k$ bits correspond to the pair a, b of numbers used to define the hash function, and the other $2k$ bits to nodes i, j that represent a possible edge in the graph. For a given node u we will represent the bits of its identifier by $u_{4k-1}, \ldots, u_0$ and the corresponding pieces by i_u, j_u, a_u, b_u.

The algorithm is divided into three phases. In the first phase, each node computes the contribution of a possible edge (i_u, j_u) to the labeling obtained by the hash function determined by a_u, b_u, and stores it in its variable h.

The second phase takes place in each subhypercube defined by fixing the first two components, notice that in each subhypercube we have stored all values produced by the corresponding hash function. Next we compute the sum of all the values stored in its nodes in the element $(0, 0, a, b)$. To do so, for $1 \leq r \leq 2k$, each node that has identifier satisfying $u_{4k-1} = \cdots = u_{4k-r+1} = 0$ and $u_{4k-r} = 1$ sends its h value to the processor that differs in the rth bit. Each node that has identifier such that $u_{4k-1} = \cdots = u_{4k-r+1} = 0$ and $u_{2k-r} = 0$ receives a value h that accumulates to its h value.

In the third phase we compute the maximum of the values stored in the hypercube $(0, 0, a, b)$. And this can be implemented as phase 2, using the other $2k$ bits, but computing maximum instead of adding. Thus at the end of the third phase processor $(0, 0, 0, 0)$ will have the value of the maximum cut in the small space; if at the same time we compute the maximum and keep the identifier of the node that contained this number, we will also compute the labeling that gives the approximate cut.

Each phase of the algorithm uses $O(\log n)$ time, and the hypercube has $O(n^4)$ processors, and thus the given implementation is as efficient as the one described for the PRAM.

There have been different proposed modes of parallel computation, other than the PRAM; the *BSP* of Valiant [Val90], or the LogP model of Culler et al. [CKP+93], among other models. However, we feel that from the point of view of dissecting the structural characteristics that made a problem easy to parallelize, the classical PRAM theory does the job well, it is simple to manipulate and can be implemented on a real parallel machine with little increase in resources.

2

Basic Concepts

In the previous chapter, we gave a brief introduction to the topic of parallel approximability. We keep the discussion at an intuitive level, trying to give the feeling of the main ideas behind parallel approximability. In this chapter, we are going to review in a more formal setting the basic definitions about PRAM computations and approximation that we shall use through the text. We will also introduce the tools and notation needed. In any case, this chapter will not be a deep study of these topics. There exists a large body of literature for the reader who wishes to go further in the theory of PRAM computation, among others the books by Akl [Akl89], Gibbons and Rytter [GR88], Reif [Rei93] and JáJá [JaJ92]. There are also excellent short surveys on this topic, we just mention the one by Karp and Ramachandran [KR90] and the collection of surveys from the ALCOM school in Warwick [GS93]. In a similar way, many survey papers and lecture notes have been written on the topic of approximability, among others the Doctoral Dissertation of V. Kann [Kan92] with a recent update on the appendix of problems [CK95], the lecture notes of R. Motwani [Mot92], the survey by Ausiello et al. [ACP96] which includes a survey of non-approximability methods, the recent book edited by Hochbaum [Hoc96] and a forthcoming book by Ausiello et al. [ACG⁺96]

2.1 The PRAM Model of Computation

We begin this section by giving a formal introduction to our basic model of computation, the Parallel Random Access Machine. A **PRAM** consists of a number of sequential processors, each with its own memory, working synchronously and communicating between themselves through a common shared memory. In one step, each processor can access one memory location (for reading or writing on it), or execute a single RAM operation. Although performing the same instructions, the processors can act on different data. This is an idealized model, and can be considered as the parallel analogue of the sequential RAM.

The PRAM machines can be classified according to the protocol used to solve conflicts in access to memory. The algorithms should be dessigned to meet the requirements of the corresponding protocol. Among other models of PRAM, we have the

- EREW (Exclusive Read Exclusive Write), simultaneous access to any memory location is forbidden.
- CREW (Concurrent Read Exclusive Write), simultaneous reads are allowed, but not simultaneous writes.
- CRCW (Concurrent Read Concurrent Write), simultaneous reads and writes are allowed. In this case it is necessary to specify the protocol to solve write conflicts. The most frequently used protocols are:
  - COMMON: all processors writing into the same location write the same value.
  - ARBITRARY: any single processor participating in a simultaneous write may succeed, and the algorithm should work correctly regardless of which one succeeds.
  - PRIORITY: there is a linear ordering on the processors, and the minimum numbered processor writes its value in a concurrent write.

The different models of PRAM do not vary too widely in their computational power, the following theorem can be found in most of the basic references on PRAMs.

Theorem 2.1.1 *Any algorithm for a PRIORITY CRCW PRAM with $P(n)$ processors and running time $T(n)$ can be simulated by an EREW PRAM with $P(n)$ processors and running time $O(T(n) \times \log P(n))$. Any algorithm for a PRIORITY CRCW PRAM with p processors and running time of $T(n)$ can be simulated by a COMMON CRCW PRAM in the same time t and using $O((P(n))^2)$ processors.*

As we mentioned in Chapter 1, when discussing the complexity of parallel algorithms, we shall take into account not only the parallel time (number of steps) but also the number of processors. Given a problem Π with input size n, let $\mathcal{A}$ be a parallel algorithm that solves Π in $T(n)$ parallel time and using $P(n)$ processors. Define the **work** of $\mathcal{A}$ as the total number of operations performed by the algorithm. The work definition describes the complexity of the algorithm in terms of a sequence of unit times, where each time unit may include any number of parallel operations. The work definition allows us to simplify the details in describing parallel algorithms for the PRAM model [JaJ92].

Although the use of work avoids having to talk specifically about the number of processors, a result known as **Brent's scheduling principle** [Bre73] gives us the trade-off between processors and parallel time: Given a PRAM algorithm with $T(n)$ parallel time, $W_i(n)$ denotes the number of operations performed in unit time i, $1 \leq i \leq T(n)$, so $W(n) = \sum_{i=1}^{T(n)} W_i(n)$ is the work of the algorithm. If we simulate the algorithm by a PRAM with $P(n)$ processors, the simulation takes $W(n)/P(n) + T(n)$ parallel steps. Therefore a reduction of the number of processors will imply a slowdown on the running time of the algorithm.

Any PRAM algorithm that performs a computation with work $W(n)$ can be converted into a sequential algorithm by letting the sequential processor simulate each parallel step i in $W_i(n)$ time units. The resulting sequential algorithm has a complexity of $W(n)$ steps [JaJ92].

Let us define polylog$(n) = \bigcup_{k>0} O(\log^k n)$, and poly$(n) = \bigcup_{k>0} O(n^k)$. A problem Π with input size n is in the class **NC** if there is a PRAM algorithm for Π finishing within polylog(n) steps and using poly(n) processors ([Coo81], [Pip79]). Let us mention that historically the class NC was defined using uniform families of boolean circuits as the underlying computational model, but due to the relationship between circuits and PRAMs, the class can also be defined in terms of PRAMs ([KR90], [JaJ92], [GHR95]). Let Π be a problem for which there is a sequential lower bound of $T_s(n)$. A parallel algorithm for Π is an *optimal* parallelization if its work $W(n) = T_s(n)$.

2.2 Randomized PRAM Computation

As we have seen in Chapter 1, randomization is a useful tool in the dessign of efficient approximation algorithms; therefore it is interesting to consider the PRAM model when extended by allowing the processors to "toss coins". In this section, we give some specific concepts and tools for designing randomized parallel algorithms. For a further study of the field, we point the reader to the book by Motwani and Raghavan [MR95]. In this section, we also introduce some concepts and theorems from graph theory that will be used through all the book.

A **randomized** PRAM has access to a source of independent and unbiased random bits and each processor is assumed to have the capability of generating $O(\log n)$ bit numbers at random.

In discussing randomized acceptance we would like the PRAM to accept (reject) most of the time, note that now on a given input there is a set of possible computations, let us denote this set by $T(x)$. In general a randomized algorithm will output one of the following answers: (a) a suitable solution; (b) report that no solution exists; (c) failure, i.e., inability to determine if there is a solution.

Most of the algorithms that we shall deal with here will be of the **Monte Carlo** type (also referred to as **one-sided error**). However, in some cases we also will use **Las Vegas** type algorithms (also known as **zero-sided error**). When the problem has a solution both types of algorithms behave similarly: each type produces a solution with probability at least 1/2, and otherwise reports failure. When the input has no solution a zero-sided error algorithm reports that no solution exists with probability greater than 1/2, and otherwise reports failure, but a one-sided error algorithm always reports failure. In other words, a Las Vegas algorithm never gives the wrong answer. Formally, we have the following

Definition 2.2.1 *Let* Π *be a problem. A* **zero-sided error** *algorithm satisfies (a) If on input* x *there is a solution then the algorithm produces a solution with probability greater than 1/2 and otherwise reports failure, (b) If on input* x *there is no solution then the algorithm reports that with probability greater than 1/2 and otherwise it fails. A* **one-sided error** *algorithm satisfies (a) If on input* x *there is a solution then the algorithm produces a solution with probability greater than 1/2 and otherwise reports failure, (b) If on input* x *there is no solution then the algorithm always reports failure.*

Recall that **RP** is defined as the class of problems solved by Monte Carlo algorithms in polynomial time (see for example [BDG88]). A problem is in the class **RNC** (**ZNC**) if there is a randomized, Monte Carlo (respectively Las Vegas) type PRAM algorithm solving it within polylogarithmic time and with a polynomial bounded work. The relationship between NC and RNC is analogous to the relationship between P and RP. An important open problem is the relation between classes RNC and P. One of the most interesting problems that can be solved by a randomized parallel algorithm is the Perfect Matching problem. Let $G = (V, E)$ be an undirected graph. A subset $X \subseteq E$ is said to be a **matching** if no two edges in X are incident on the same vertex. A matching is said to be a **Perfect Matching** if it covers all the vertices in G. The Maximum Matching problem is to find a matching of maximum cardinality. When considering the problem of finding a perfect matching, often the underlying graph is a bipartite graph. A **bipartite**

graph is a graph whose set of vertices can be partitioned into two subsets V_1 and V_2 such that every edge of the graph joins V_1 with V_2. It is known that the Perfect Matching and the Maximum Matching problems are in P.

A much more involved version of the matching problem is the one in which we are given the graph $G = (V, E)$ and an integer weight $w(e)$ for each edge $e \in E$, called the weight. The Maximum Weight Matching problem is, given a weighted graph $G = (V, E)$, to find a matching of G with the largest possible sum of weights. The Maximum Weight Perfect Matching problem consists in finding a perfect matching maximizing the sum of the weights on the edges.

Historically, Karp, Upfal and Wigderson were the first ones to give an RNC algorithm for the Perfect Matching problem [KUW86]. Mulmuley, Vazirani and Vazirani provided an elegant RNC algorithm to find a perfect matching in a graph, using $O(\log^2 n)$ steps [MVV87]. Their algorithm is based on a key result, the so called Isolating Lemma. This lemma can be stated in a general way in terms of subset collections.

Definition 2.2.2 *A* **set system** (S, F) *consists of a finite set S of elements* $S = \{x_1, \ldots, x_n\}$ *and a family F of subsets of S, $F = \{S_1, \ldots, S_k\}$ with* $S_j \subseteq S$, $1 \le j \le k$. *Let us assign a weight w_j to each element $x_j \in S$ and define* $\mathrm{weight}(S_j) = \sum_{x_i \in S_j} w_i$.

Lemma 2.2.1 (Isolating Lemma) *Let (S, F) be a set system with integer weights chosen uniformly and independently from $[1, 2n]$. Then, with probability at least $1/2$, F contains a unique minimum weight set.*

Proof Fix the weights of all elements except x_i. Define the threshold x_i to be the real number a_i such that:

   (i) If $w_i \le a_i$ then x_i belongs to some minimum weight set.
  (ii) If $w_i > a_i$ then x_i is not in any minimum weight set.

Clearly if $w_i < a_i$ then x_i belongs to all minimum weight sets. The ambiguity appears when $w_i = a_i$ because then x_i belongs to some minimum weight set but not to some other minimum weight set. Then x_i is called **singular**.

But the threshold a_i was defined without reference to the weight w_i of x_i. It follows that a_i is independent of w_i. Since w_i is uniformly distributed in $[1, 2n]$, we get

$$\Pr\{w_i = a_i\} \le \frac{1}{2n}.$$

Since S has n elements we have that the probability that a singular element

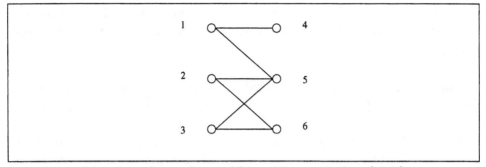

Fig. 2.1: An undirected bipartite graph $G = (V, E)$

exists is at most $n \cdot \frac{1}{2n} = 1/2$. Thus with probability at least $1/2$ no element is singular and there exists a unique minimum weight set. ☐

Notice that by choosing the weights in the range $[1, 2n]$ we make the probability of existence of a unique minimum weight set strictly greater than $1/2$.

Let F be the set of perfect matchings in a graph $G = (V, E)$ that has $|E| = m$. If each edge weight is assigned a random integer weight in $[1, 2m]$ then by the Isolating Lemma the probability that there is a unique perfect matching of minimum weight is strictly greater than $1/2$. The RNC algorithm for perfect matching also uses the so called Tutte matrix.

Definition 2.2.3 *Let $G = (V, E)$ be a bipartite graph with vertex set $V = \{1, 2, \ldots, 2n\}$. The* **Tutte matrix** $A = (a_{ij})$ *of G is defined by,*

$$
a_{ij} = \begin{cases} x_{ij} & \text{if } (i,j) \in E \text{ and } i < j, \\ -x_{ij} & \text{if } (i,j) \in E \text{ and } i > j, \\ 0 & \text{if } (i,j) \notin E, \end{cases}
$$

where x_{ij} are indeterminates.

Notice that for any simple graph, its adjacency matrix is symmetric, while its Tutte matrix is skew-symmetric. For instance, the Tutte matrix corresponding to the graph in Figure 2.1 is the following:

$$
\begin{pmatrix}
0 & 0 & 0 & x_{14} & x_{15} & 0 \\
0 & 0 & 0 & 0 & x_{25} & x_{26} \\
0 & 0 & 0 & 0 & x_{35} & x_{36} \\
-x_{14} & 0 & 0 & 0 & 0 & 0 \\
-x_{15} & -x_{25} & -x_{35} & 0 & 0 & 0 \\
0 & -x_{26} & -x_{36} & 0 & 0 & 0
\end{pmatrix}
$$

The following well known result gives the relation between the existence of perfect matchings and the determinant of the Tutte matrix [Tut47] (see also [LP86]).

Theorem 2.2.2 (Tutte's Theorem) *A graph G has a perfect matching if the determinant of its corresponding Tutte matrix is not identically zero.*

It is well known that it is possible to test in RNC whether a multivariate polynomial is not identically zero [Sch80]. Using the above results, Mulmuley, Vazirani and Vazirani gave Algorithm 7 for determining whether a graph has a perfect matching. Recall that the *adjoint* of an $n \times n$ matrix M is an $n \times n$ matrix whose (i, j) entry has been replaced by $(-1)^{i+j} \det(M_{ij})$, where M_{ij} is the submatrix obtained from M by deleting the jth row and the ith column. All the above steps can be computed by a CREW PRAM,

---

PERFECTMATCHING (G)

1 In parallel, for each edge $e = (i, j)$ assign uniformly and randomly a weight between $w_{ij} \in [0, 2m]$.

2 Form the Tutte matrix of G. Replace each x_{ij} by $2^{w_{ij}}$. Let B be the new matrix.

3 Compute in NC the determinant of B and the adjoint of B.

4 Let 2^w be the highest power of 2 that divides $\det(B)$. Then w is the weight of the unique minimum weight perfect matching.

5 In parallel, for each edge $e = (i, j) \in E$ compute $m(e) := \frac{|B_{ij}| 2^{w_{ij}}}{2^w}$.

6 Let M be the set of edges for which $m(e)$ is odd. If $|M| = n/2$, then output M.

Algorithm 7: Perfect Matching in RNC.

in $O(\log^2 n)$ steps and using a polynomial number of processors.

Algorithm 7 together with the reductions given by Karp, Upfal and Wigderson [KUW86] proves the following result.

Theorem 2.2.3 *The following problems involving matchings can be solved by a randomized PRAM machine, in $O(\log^2 n)$ steps and using a polynomial* *number of processors.*

- Perfect Matching.
- Maximum Weight Matching *in a graph whose edge weights are given in unary notation.*
- Maximum Cardinality Matching.

Karloff gave two algorithms for transferring the above Monte Carlo algorithm into a Las Vegas algorithm, thus establishing membership in ZNC, for all the problems mentioned in the above theorem, and still using $O(\log^2 n)$ parallel steps [Kar86].

2.3 P-Completeness

In complexity theory it is customary to define classes of problems with equivalent computational difficulty. The class NP captures the idea of difficult problems, where given a conjectured solution, we can prove deterministically in polynomial time that the conjecture is indeed a solution to the problem. Recall that P is the class of problems that can be solved by deterministic algorithms in polynomial time, and **LOG** is the class of problems that can be solved by a deterministic algorithm, using logarithmic space (see for example [BDG88], [GJ79], [Pap94]).

Complexity classes cluster problems with equivalent computational difficulty. To classify problems we use a notion of reducibility. Informally a problem Π_1 is *reducible* to a problem Π_2 if there exists a transformation from instances of Π_1 to instances of Π_2, such that the transformation can be computed with the weakest computational resources possible with respect to the class under consideration, and given an algorithm $\mathcal{A}$ to solve Π_2, $\mathcal{A}$ together with the transformation will produce an algorithm that solves Π_1. The formalization of reduction between problems is done by codifying the problems as languages over a finite alphabet, and defining the reducibility function over the corresponding subset of words. Notice that a decision problem corresponds to deciding whether a word representing the input belongs to a given language or not ([GJ79], [BDG88], [Pap94]). We refer the reader to those references for the formal definitions of many–one reduction.

The reducibility between problems is denoted by $\leq_{\mathcal{F}}$, where $\mathcal{F}$ denotes the resources and machine we are using to compute the reducibility. For instance, if we are using $\mathcal{F} = \text{LOG}$ we are requiring that the reduction must be computed by a deterministic Turing machine using at most a logarithmic bounded amount of space. If $\mathcal{F} = \text{NC}$, we require that the reduction must be computed by a PRAM in a polylogarithmic number of steps and using a polynomial number of processors.

The class NP-complete of most difficult NP problems was defined in an effort to prove that not all problems in NP are likely to be in P. To show an NP problem is NP-complete, we reduce in polynomial time a known NP-complete problem to the problem under consideration. For a very nice exposition of the theory of NP-completeness, see the book of Garey and Johnson [GJ79]. The optimization version of problems where we are required to find the explicit solution belongs to the class Δ_p^2, a higher class in the polynomial time hierarchy (see for example [BDG88]).

In terms of decision problems, many–one reductions allow us to compare the complexity of decision problems, whenever the subclass of functions chosen to perform the reduction satisfies some good properties relatively to the class under study. The composition of reductions of the same type results in a new reduction. Therefore the reducibility induces an equivalence relation on the class where it is defined, allowing us to identify the hardest sets in the class. More formally, we have the following.

Definition 2.3.1 *A problem* Π *is* **hard** *for the class* C *under reduction* $\leq_{\mathcal{F}}$ *iff for all* Π_1 *in the class* C, $\Pi_1 \leq_{\mathcal{F}} \Pi$. *Further,* Π *is complete for the class* C *under* $\leq_{\mathcal{F}}$ *iff* Π *is hard for* C *under* $\leq_{\mathcal{F}}$ *and* $\Pi \in$ C.

Two of the most used reductions are the ones we already briefly mentioned, based on functions computed in log-space and functions computed in NC. We denote them by $\leq_{LOG}$ and $\leq_{NC}$ respectively [Pap94]. Since all log-space transformations are computable in NC we have that $A \leq_{LOG} B$ implies $A \leq_{NC} B$. Therefore if a language is complete for P under log-space or NC reductions then the language is in NC if and only if P = NC. At the present $\leq_{LOG}$ appears to be a weaker notion of reducibility than $\leq_{NC}$.

The usual method of proving a problem P-complete is to show that it lies in P and that some standard P-complete problem is reducible to it. The most often used P-complete problem for this purpose is the Circuit Value problem and its variations. In the Circuit Value problem the input is a description of a boolean circuit together with an input assignment. The objective is to compute the value of the output gate. The different restrictions on the set of gates allowed and on the topology of the circuit determine various kinds of Circuit Value problems. The input is a description of a circuit consisting of:

(i) Input "gates" that indicate a certain wire as an input. The input wire can be designated to hold constant 0 or 1. We also designate each input gate to be associated with some input variable name.

(ii) Computational "gates" with some number of input wires and some output wires. A designated boolean function determines the output value from the input value or values.

In general we speak of AND, OR and NOT gates, but we could also consider circuits composed of gates from any finite repertoire of boolean functions; each repertoire defines another family of Circuit Value problems. We assume the description of the circuit is a sequence of gates $(\alpha_1, \ldots, \alpha_n)$, where the input of each gate α_i consists only of gates with numbers less than i. Finally we may assume without loss of generality that the output of the last gate α_n is the circuit's output. The most general Circuit Value problem is the following.

Definition 2.3.2 *Given an encoding of a boolean circuit constructed from computational gates NOT and gates AND and OR with arbitrary fan-in and fan-out, together with an input assignment.* **The Circuit Value problem** *is to determine whether the output is 0 or 1.*

The following classical result due to Ladner [Lad75] can be found in many standard books ([BDG88], [GHR95]).

Theorem 2.3.1 (Ladner) *The* Circuit Value *problem is* P-*complete.*

We sometimes want to restrict circuits to gates with limited fan-in (fan-out), especially 2, or to restrict the circuit's topology. The topology restrictions considered here are planarity and alternation. We shall consider the following circuit classes:

- *Binary circuit.* A boolean circuit whose gate repertoire consists of NOT, two-input AND and two-input OR.
- *Monotone circuit.* A circuit restricted to two-input AND and OR gates.
- *NAND circuit.* A circuit restricted to two input and two output NAND gates.
- *Fan-out 2 monotone circuit.* A monotone circuit restricted to two-output AND and OR gates.
- A circuit is **planar** if we can draw it as a planar graph, whose nodes are gates and whose edges are the wires that connect the gates.
- A monotone circuit is **alternating** if it is divided into levels with all gates in a level of the same type, the levels alternate between AND and OR gates, further inputs to a level are taken only from the previous level.
- A *fan-out 2 monotone alternating circuit* is an alternating monotone circuit limited to two-output gates.

From standard results given among others in [Lad75], [GHR95], [BDG88] we have

Theorem 2.3.2 *The* Circuit Value *problem is* P-*complete for any of the following circuit classes: binary, monotone, fan-out* 2 *monotone, planar, alternating, and fan-out* 2 *monotone alternating.*

2.4 Approximation Algorithms

Let us review formally the notion of approximation algorithm, this notion is independent of the particular implementation of the algorithm, and thus is common to both parallel and sequential approximation theories.

Definition 2.4.1 *An* **optimization problem** Π *is a triple* $(D, S(x), \kappa)$ *where*

- *D is the set of input instances,*
- *$S(x)$ is the set of all feasible solutions for each instance $x \in D$,*
- *κ is a cost function $\kappa : S(x) \rightarrow \mathbb{R}$ assigning a real value to each solution.*

We say that a problem is a **maximization problem** *if given an input $x \in D$, we wish to find an optimal solution $s_o(x)$ such that for every solution $s \in S(x)$, $\kappa(s_o(x)) \geq \kappa(s)$. We denote by $\text{Opt}_\Pi(x)$ the value $\kappa(s_o(x))$. In a similar way we can define a* **minimization problem**.

For the Maximum Cut problem defined in Chapter 1, D is the set of graphs. Given a graph x, with vertex set V and edge set E,

$$S(x) = \{\{V_1, V_2\}|V_1 \cup V_2 = V \text{ and } V_1 \cap V_2 = \emptyset\},$$

and for any feasible solution $s \in S(x)$, $\kappa(s)$ is the number of edges between V_1 and V_2.

Let **NPO** be the class of optimization problems whose decision version is in NP. Therefore the Maximum Cut problem belongs to the class NPO.

Many problems in NPO that have been proved to be hard to solve in polynomial time have efficient approximations algorithms. An approximation algorithm $\mathcal{A}$ to a problem Π takes some input $x \in D$ to the problem, and gives a solution in the set of feasible solutions. We will denote by $\mathcal{A}(x)$ the **cost** of the feasible solution produced by $\mathcal{A}$ on input x.

There are different kinds of approximation algorithms depending on three considerations: "how close" can we get to the optimal solution; what kind of algorithm are we considering (sequential or parallel); and what resource bounds do we impose on the algorithm. To formalize the concept of closeness, we need to measure the error of a given solution.

Definition 2.4.2 *A solution s to an instance x of an NPO problem Π has* **error** $\epsilon(x, s)$ *if*

$$\frac{1}{1 + \epsilon(x, s)} \leq \frac{\kappa\,(s)}{\text{Opt}_\Pi(x)} \leq 1 + \epsilon(x, s).$$

Therefore we can measure the approximation quality of an algorithm by measuring the error of the computed solution. Note that $\epsilon(x, s) \geq 0$.

Definition 2.4.3 *Given an optimization problem Π, and an approximation algorithm $\mathcal{A}$ for the problem:*

(i) *We say that $\mathcal{A}$ has a* **relative error** $\epsilon_\mathcal{A}(x) = \epsilon(x, s)$, *where s is the solution computed by $\mathcal{A}$ on input x.*

(ii) *Given an optimization problem Π, the* **performance ratio** *for an approximation algorithm $\mathcal{A}$ with respect to an input x is defined by*

$$R_\mathcal{A}(x) = \max\left\{\frac{\text{Opt}_\Pi(x)}{\mathcal{A}(x)}, \frac{\mathcal{A}(x)}{\text{Opt}_\Pi(x)}\right\}.$$

Notice that both definitions apply to maximization and minimization problems at all levels of approximability. Moreover from the definitions it follows than for an instance x of a given problem, for any approximation algorithm $\mathcal{A}$ we get

$$R_\mathcal{A}(x) \leq 1 + \epsilon_\mathcal{A}(x).$$

Given a function $\epsilon : \mathbb{N} \to (0, 1]$, we say that a given algorithm $\mathcal{A}$ approximates within ϵ, or it is an ϵ-**approximation**, to an optimization problem Π, if for every input x,

$$R_\mathcal{A}(x) \leq \frac{1}{\epsilon(|x|)}.$$

Definition 2.4.4 *Given an approximation algorithm $\mathcal{A}$ for a problem Π its* **absolute performance ratio** *is defined to be*

$$R_\mathcal{A} = \inf\{r \geq 1 \mid R_\mathcal{A}(x) \leq r \text{ for all } x \in D\}.$$

For some problems, there may be inputs where the value of the optimal solution is small, and for a given approximation algorithm its performance may differ very little from the optimal, but the absolute ratio appears to be very large. To avoid this abnormality it has been customary to introduce an asymptotic measure of the performace ratio.

Definition 2.4.5 *Given an approximation algorithm* $\mathcal{A}$ *for a problem* Π *its* **asymptotic performance ratio** *is defined to be*

$$R_{\mathcal{A}}^{\infty} = \inf_{x \in D} \{r \mid \exists n_0 \, \forall x \in D \, (\mathrm{Opt}(x) \geq n_0 \Rightarrow R_{\mathcal{A}}(x) \leq r)\}.$$

With these definitions of the measure of the approximation, we can introduce the most usual classes of problems according to their degree of approximability beginning with those problems that could be approximated as close to the optimal solution as we wish.

2.5 Parallel Approximation Classes

In this section we review some sequential approximation classes, and introduce their parallel counterparts.

Definition 2.5.1 *An* **approximation scheme** *for a given problem* Π *is a family of algorithms* $\{\mathcal{A}_\epsilon | \epsilon > 0\}$ *such that* $R_{\mathcal{A}_\epsilon} \leq 1 + \epsilon$. *This definition could be stated in an almost equivalent way in terms of a single algorithm* $\mathcal{A}$ *which takes an input* (x, ϵ) *and such that* $R_{\mathcal{A}}(x, \epsilon) \leq 1 + \epsilon$.

The class of problems solved by a deterministic approximation scheme within a polynomial (in $|x|$) number of steps is called the class **PTAS** of **Polynomial Time Approximation Scheme** problems. If $\{\mathcal{A}_\epsilon\}$ are PRAM algorithms working within a polylogarithmic (in $|x|$) number of steps and using a polynomial number of operations, we get the class **NCAS** of problems with **NC Approximation Schemes**.

We can consider also the asymptotic versions of these classes. The class **PTAS**$^\infty$ consists of problems for which there is a family of deterministic algorithms $\{\mathcal{A}_\epsilon\}$ that take as input x and produce a solution in a polynomial (in $|x|$) number of steps, within $1 + \epsilon$ of the optimum, as $|x| \to \infty$. The class **NCAS**$^\infty$ is defined in a similar way.

Problems in PTAS (NCAS) have a drawback, they may have a running time polynomial in the size of the input, but exponential in $1/\epsilon$. An example is the Maximum Independent Set problem: given a graph, find the maximum set of vertices that are pairwise nonadjacent. For general graphs and planar graphs, the problem is NP-complete. For planar graphs the problem of finding a Maximum Independent Set has a PTAS running in $O(\frac{n 8^{1/\epsilon}}{\epsilon})$. To avoid this inconvenience, we require the running time to be bounded by a polynomial in both the size of the input and the error ϵ.

Given an optimization problem Π, a **Full Approximation Scheme** for Π is a family of algorithms $\{A_\epsilon\}$ such that $R_{A_\epsilon} \leq 1 + \epsilon$. If the algorithms are sequential and run in polynomial time in $(|x|, 1/\epsilon)$, then the problem belongs to the class of **Full Polynomial Time Approximation Schemes**, **FPTAS**. If the algorithms in the family are PRAM and run in polylogarithmic time in $(|x|, 1/\epsilon)$ and with a polynomial (in $|x|$ and $1/\epsilon$) number of processors, the problem belongs to the class **FNCAS** of problems having a **Full NC Approximation Scheme**. Again as with the previous classes we have analogous asymptotic versions. Let **FPTAS**$^\infty$ be the class of problems for which there is a family of deterministic algorithms $\{A_\epsilon\}$ that take as input x and produce a solution within $1 + \epsilon$ of the optimum, in a polynomial (in $|x|$ and $1/\epsilon$) number of steps, asymptotically when $|x| \to \infty$. The class **FNCAS**$^\infty$ is defined in a similar way. The class FPTAS has been very well studied. In the next sections, we shall present results about the classes FNCAS and FNCAS$^\infty$.

Frequently it is not possible to get so close to the solution as is the case with problems in previous classes. Still there are interesting degrees of approximations and classifications for problems not fitting in the previously defined schemes. To capture one such result we define the class APX. A problem Π is in the class **APX** if there is a polynomial (in $|x|$) time algorithm that c-approximates Π for some constant $c \geq 1$. A problem Π is in the class **NCX** if there is a parallel algorithm running in a polylogarithmic (in $|x|$) number of steps and with a polynomial (in $|x|$) number of processors, such that it c-approximates Π, for some constant $c \geq 1$. The relationship between sequential and parallel approximation classes is given in Figure 2.2.

There are some problems that seem very hard to approximate. The most celebrated of the non-approximability results is the one by Arora et al. [ALM+92]

Theorem 2.5.1 *There is a constant $c \in \mathbb{R}^+$ such that given a graph G with a sufficiently large number n of nodes, the problem of finding a Maximum Independent Set of nodes in G cannot be approximated in P within n^c, unless* P = NP.

The proof of the theorem uses the theory of Interactive Proof Systems, and it has given rise to a very exciting field of research about non-approximability.

For a recent survey on sequential non-approximability, see the paper by Bellare [Bel96] and Section 5 of [ACP96].

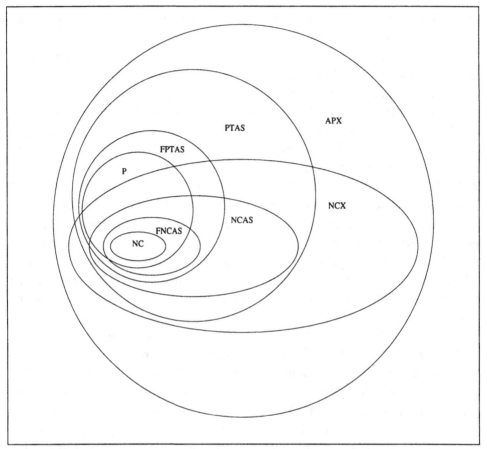

Fig. 2.2: Parallel versus sequential approximation classes

2.6 Approximation Preserving Reductions

In fact, there are several other problems that share the same characteristic of
non-approximability as the Maximum Independent Set problem. Therefore,
it seems natural to define classes of problems that show equivalent degrees of
approximability. To do so we need the concept of approximation preserving
reduction. The usual many–one reduction used for NP-completeness does
not preserve approximability properties. There are many kinds of approximation preserving reductions depending on what kind of approximation we
have. The general idea is that an approximation preserving reduction f
from an optimization problem Π_1 into an optimization problem Π_2 must
transform each instance of Π_1 in an instance of Π_2 in such a way that it
also transforms each solution of the particular instance of Π_2 into a solution of the corresponding instance to Π_1 and somehow preserves the "ratio

of approximation" of each solution [ADP80]. The most widely used reduction is the *L*-reducibility of Papadimitriou and Yannakakis [PY91]. However, it is known that for some approximability classes, unless P = NP ∩ co-NP, the *L*-reduction is not approximation preserving [CKST95]. The introduction in this last reference contains a very nice comparative study of the different kinds of reducibilities used in dealing with approximation classes.

We will use the *E*-reduction introduced by Khanna, Motwani, Sudan and Vazirani [KMSV94], with slight modification to change the resources required to compute the functions, so it can be appropriate to our parallel complexity classes.

Definition 2.6.1 *Let Π_1 and Π_2 be two optimization problems. We say that Π_1 is E-reducible to Π_2 if there is a pair of functions f and g computable in logarithmic space, and a positive constant c satisfying the following properties:*

- *f transforms instances of Π_1 into instances of Π_2.*
- *if s is a solution of $f(x)$ then $g(x,s)$ is a solution to x such that $\epsilon(x, g(x,s)) \leq c\epsilon(f(x), s)$.*

Intuitively, f transforms instances of Π_1 into instances of Π_2 as in a canonical reduction, and g maps solutions for the transformed problem into solutions for the original one, maintaining the "quality" of the solution, in the sense that the error for Π_1 should be linearly related to the error for Π_2. E-reductions are used to obtain approximation algorithms, for problem Π_1, using approximation algorithms for problem Π_2 preserving the quality of the approximation. (See Figure 2.3.)

Since logarithmic space computable functions can be composed using only logarithmic space, *E*-reducibility is transitive. Another good property of this reducibility is that it preserves NC approximability within a constant factor, that is, if a problem Π_2 can be approximated in NC up to a constant factor, and Π_1 is *E*-reducible to Π_2, then Π_1 also has an NC constant factor approximation algorithm. The idea to approximate the optimum solution of an instance x of Π_1 is to use the functions f and g of the *E*-reduction in the following way: first transform x into an instance $f(x)$ of Π_2, and compute an approximate solution $s \in S(f(x))$ for $f(x)$; finally transform s into a solution $g(x,s)$ of x. By the definition of the *E*-reducibility, $g(x,s)$ is an approximation of x. Also, all the computations done in the process (f,g) as well as the approximation to $f(x)$ can be performed in NC.

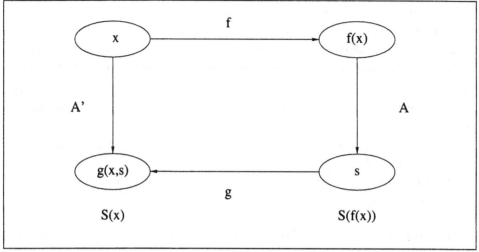

Fig. 2.3: E-reduction scheme

2.7 Pseudo-NC Algorithms and Approximation

We are interested in the complexity of subproblems obtained by placing restrictions on the magnitude of the numbers which form part of a problem instance. Those restrictions will be defined in terms of two encoding functions. Given an optimization problem Π, define Length : $D \to \mathbb{Z}^+$ and Max : $D \to \mathbb{Z}^+$. The function Length is defined in order to map an instance x to an integer that corresponds to the length of a description of x, up to a polynomial, while Max will be the largest positive integer in x, or 0 if x does not contain positive integers. We furthermore require that those functions should be computed in NC, that is, given any reasonable encoding scheme for Π, there must exist an NC algorithm that outputs the values of Length(x) and Max(x). Note that an encoding of Max(x) may only need $\log(\text{Max}(x))$ bits, so when large numbers are allowed we can easily have Length $= O(\log \text{Max})$.

As an example, an instance of the Circuit Value problem has no numbers at all, so in this case we get Length equal to the number of gates in a given circuit and Max equal to 0. The Linear Inequalities problem is defined as, given a linear system of inequalities, how to determine whether there is a rational vector that satisfies all the inequalities. When we look at an instance of the Linear Inequalities problem there are two types of numbers, the number of variables and the coefficients. The length of an input description should be the number of variables times the logarithm of the maximum coefficient value. Then Length can be defined as the number of variables, and Max as the maximum value of the coefficients.

Definition 2.7.1 *An algorithm that solves a problem* Π *will be called a* **pseudo-NC algorithm** *if it uses a number of processors bounded above by a polynomial in* Length *and if its time complexity is bounded above by a polylogarithmic function of the two variables* Length *and* Max.

By definition, any NC algorithm is also a pseudo-NC algorithm, because its complexity is only related to the Length function.

Definition 2.7.2 *We say that an optimization problem* $\Pi = (D, S(x), \kappa)$ *is a* **number problem** *if there exists no polynomial* p *such that for all instances* x *in* D $\mathrm{Max}(x) \leq p(\mathrm{Length}(x))$.

It is clear that the Circuit Value problem is not a number problem, while the Linear Inequalities problem is a number problem. As a consequence of the previous definition we have

Lemma 2.7.1 *If* Π *is P-complete and* Π *is not a number problem then* Π *cannot be solved by a pseudo-NC algorithm unless* P=NC.

Thus assuming that P≠NC, the only P-complete problems that are candidates to be solved by pseudo-NC algorithms are those that are number problems. For any problem Π and any polynomial p, let Π_p denote the subproblem of Π obtained by restricting Π to only those instances x that satisfy $\mathrm{Max}(x) \leq p(\mathrm{Length}(x))$. Notice that with this restriction Π_p is not a number problem for every polynomial p, and under the assumption that Max and Length can be computed in NC, we have

Lemma 2.7.2 *For any polynomial* p, *if* Π *is solvable by a pseudo-NC algorithm then* Π_p *is solvable by an* NC *algorithm.*

The above lemma shows that P-complete number problems may have quite a different behavior when we look at polynomial restrictions. In order to reflect this fact we set the following definition.

Definition 2.7.3 *We say that a problem* Π *is* **P-complete in the strong sense** *if* Π *belongs to* P *and there exists a polynomial* p *for which* Π_p *is P-complete.*

In particular if Π is not a number problem then Π is P-complete in the strong sense, so the Circuit Value problem is P-complete in the strong sense. We have the following generalization of Lemma 2.7.1.

Lemma 2.7.3 *If* Π *is P-complete in the strong sense then* Π *cannot be solved by a pseudo-NC algorithm unless* $P = NC$.

The existence of Full NC Approximation Schemes, for integer valued optimization problems, relates to the existence of pseudo-NC algorithms when the value of the function Opt is bounded by a polynomial in Length and Max.

Theorem 2.7.4 *Let* Π *be an integer valued optimization problem. If there exists a two-variable polynomial* q *such that for all instances* $x \in D$, $\mathrm{Opt}(x)$ *is bounded above by* $q(\mathrm{Length}(x), \mathrm{Max}(x))$, *then the existence of a Full NC Approximation Scheme for* Π *implies the existence of a pseudo-NC algorithm for* Π.

Proof Suppose that $\mathcal{A}$ is such a scheme for Π. The corresponding optimization algorithm $\mathcal{B}$ proceeds as follows: Given an instance x, set

$$\epsilon = q\left(\mathrm{Length}(x), \mathrm{Max}(x)\right)$$

and apply $\mathcal{A}$ to the instance x and ϵ. Then, in pseudo-NC, $\mathcal{A}_\epsilon$ finds a candidate solution for x satisfying

$$R_{\mathcal{A}_\epsilon(x)} \le 1 + 1/\epsilon.$$

Let us assume that Π is a maximization problem. Then we have

$$\mathrm{Opt}(x) \le (1 + 1/\epsilon)\mathcal{A}_\epsilon(x)$$

or

$$\mathrm{Opt}(x) - \mathcal{A}_\epsilon(x) \le \mathcal{A}_\epsilon(x)/\epsilon \le \mathrm{Opt}(x)/\epsilon < 1.$$

But since all solutions are integers we have $\mathcal{A}_\epsilon(x) = \mathrm{Opt}(x)$. So $\mathcal{B}$ finds an optimal solution and is a pseudo-NC algorithm for Π. $\square$

Corollary 2.7.5 *Let* Π *be an integer valued optimization problem satisfying the hypothesis of the previous theorem. If* Π *is P-hard in the strong sense, then* Π *cannot be solved by a Full NC Approximation Scheme unless* $P = NC$.

On the other hand a proof of P-completeness for a decision problem obtained from an optimization problem allows us to obtain some knowledge about the difficulty of finding approximation algorithms for some absolute performance ratios.

Theorem 2.7.6 *Let* Π *be an optimization problem having all solution values in* $\mathbb{Z}^+$, *and suppose that for some fixed* $k \in \mathbb{Z}^+$ *the decision problem "Given* $x \in D$ *is* $\mathrm{Opt}(x) \le k$*?" is P-hard. Then if* $P \ne NC$, *no NC approximation algorithm* $\mathcal{A}$ *for* Π *can satisfy* $R_{\mathcal{A}} < 1 + 1/k$, *and* Π *cannot be solved by an NC approximation scheme.*

Proof Suppose that Π is a minimization problem and that there is an NC approximation algorithm with $R_{\mathcal{A}} \le 1 + 1/k$, then we have:

If $\mathrm{Opt}(x) > k$ then $\mathcal{A}(x) \ge \mathrm{Opt}(x) > k$.

If $\mathrm{Opt}(x) \le k$ then $\mathcal{A}(x) < (1 + 1/k)\mathrm{Opt}(x) \le k + 1$, but as the solutions are required to be integers, we have that $\mathcal{A}(x) \le k$.

So $\mathrm{Opt}(x) \le k$ iff $\mathcal{A}(x) \le k$, and we can solve a P-complete problem in NC. $\square$

3

Extremal Graph Properties

An interesting question in graph theory is to find whether a given graph contains a vertex induced subgraph satisfying a certain property. We shall consider the special case where the property depends only on the value of a certain parameter that can take (positive) integer values. Such properties are described as **weighted properties**. For a given graph $G = (V, E)$, $G' \subseteq G$ means that G' is a vertex induced subgraph of G. The generic Induced Subgraph of High Weight problem (ISHW) consists in, given a graph $G = (V, E)$, a weighted property W on the set of graphs, and an integer k, to decide if G contains a vertex induced subgraph H such that $W(H) \geq k$. A first concrete example of the Induced Subgraph of High Weight problem is the case when W is the minimum degree of a graph. This instance of the problem is known as the High Degree Subgraph problem (HDS). Historically, this is the first problem shown to be P-complete and approximated in parallel ([AM86] and [HS87]). Another instance of the Induced Subgraph of High Weight is the case when W is the vertex (or edge) connectivity of G. These problems are known as the High Vertex Connected Subgraph problem (HVCS) (respectively the High Edge Connected Subgraph problem (HECS)). As we shall show in Chapter 8, these problems are also P-complete for any $k \geq 3$.

Anderson and Mayr studied the High Degree Subgraph problem and found that the approximability of the problem exhibits a threshold type behavior. This behavior implies that below a certain value of the absolute performance ratio, it remains P-complete, even for fixed value k. On the other hand, above that ratio there are NC approximation algorithms for the problem, and thus it belongs to the class NCX. Similar results were found by Kirousis, Serna and Spirakis for the High Vertex Connected Subgraph and the High Edge Connected Subgraph problems ([KSS93], [Ser90]). Not much progress has been made on other weighted properties, with the exception of the linkage of a graph. The High Linkage Subgraph problem was studied by Kirousis and Thilikos, and it exhibits similar threshold properties as the problems described above [KT96].

It remains an open problem to study the NC approximability for the High Degree Subgraph problem and the High Vertex Connected Subgraph problem for the case $\epsilon = 1/2$. Also an open problem is to sharpen the threshold for the other two problems. Another interesting question is that of computing the subgraph of high weight. The only known result is for the case of the High Degree Subgraph, for this problem Andreev et al. prove that the sequential algorithm that follows from the extremal graph result is P-complete [ACC+95].

In this chapter we will develop a general theory that can be used to place all these problems in the class NCX.

3.1 The Induced Subgraph of High Weight is in NCX

The methodology we present in this section applies to weighted properties of graphs whose weight increases when the edges of G increase. Such properties are monotone with respect to edge addition. Let us formalize this idea.

Definition 3.1.1 *Let W be a weighted property of undirected graphs. Property W is called a **linear extremal graph property (LEP)** when it satisfies the condition that given a graph G with n vertices and m edges, G has a vertex induced subgraph H with*

$$W(H) \geq \left\lceil \sigma \frac{m + \gamma n + \alpha}{n + \beta} \right\rceil$$

where $\sigma, \alpha, \gamma, \beta$ are constants, and $\sigma \leq 1$.

Extremal graph theory can be useful to prove that a given property W is LEP. We will prove in the next section that several weighted properties satisfy these conditions.

Consider an instance of the Induced Subgraph of High Weight problem with W being an LEP. We define a vertex elimination procedure whose goal is to produce a dense enough subgraph of G to exploit the LEP property for our approximation purposes. Given a graph G with n vertices, and k, ϵ, Algorithm 8 computes a subgraph H with $W(H) \geq k$ or the empty set.

Using Algorithm 8 as a function we can now produce the fast approximation procedure FAST for a graph G with n vertices, given as Algorithm 9.

To prove the correctness of the procedure, we need first a technical lemma,

TEST (G, k, ϵ)
1   **while** $G \neq \emptyset$ **do**
2        $W := \{v \in V | \text{degree of } (v) < k\}$;
3   **if** $|W| < (1 - \epsilon/\sigma)n$ **then** return **true**
4   **else** $G := G - W$;
5   return **false**

Algorithm 8: Vertex elimination procedure

FAST (G, ϵ)
1   **for all** $0 \leq k \leq n$ **pardo**
2   TEST (G, k, ϵ);
3   select the highest k which returns **true**

Algorithm 9: Parallel Approximation to ISHW

Lemma 3.1.1 *Whenever* TEST(G, k, ϵ) *returns* **true**, *then there exists an induced subgraph* H *with* $W(H) \geq k\epsilon$.

Proof Suppose that at a certain moment during the computation of TEST, the remaining graph has q vertices, and the procedure returns **true**. This means that there are fewer than $(1 - 2\epsilon/\sigma)q$ vertices of degree less than k. So there must be at least $q2\epsilon/\sigma$ vertices of degree at least k, and thus there would have to be at least $2qk\epsilon/2\sigma$ edges in the graph. As W is an LEP, the remaining graph has a vertex induced subgraph with $W \geq k\epsilon$.   □

Now we can prove the main result in this chapter,

Theorem 3.1.2 *For LEP properties of a graph, the corresponding High Weight Subgraph problem is in* NCX.

Proof We must show that the procedure FAST achieves an approximation of the Induced Subgraph of High Weight problem in NCX. Let us consider the highest value of k in the range $[0, n]$ for which TEST returns **true**. In this case we get a value k for which G has an induced subgraph H with $W(H) \geq M(G)\epsilon$, where $M(G)$ is the highest possible of the W values on the induced subgraphs, but there is no subgraph with value of W greater than $M(G) + 1$.

Regarding the parallel time and work of the algorithms, we use a CRCW PRAM. Then to count the number of iterations in the loop of TEST, note that if the loop does not terminate, it means that at least a fraction $(1-2\epsilon/\sigma)$ of the vertices are removed. Therefore after i iterations, at most $(2\epsilon/\sigma)^i n$ vertices remain in the graph. If $i > \log_{(2\epsilon/\sigma)}(n)$ then we can assure that TEST would finish, therefore $O(\log n)$ iterations suffice, with a work of $O(m \log n)$.

To determine the degree of each vertex, we also need a parallel time of $O(\log n)$ with a work $O(m \log n)$. Moreover, the removal of the vertices with degree less than k and of their incident edges can be done by a CRCW PRAM in constant parallel time and work $O(mn)$. □

3.2 Examples of Linear Extremal Graph Properties

Let us start with some definitions. For a given graph G the **degree** of any vertex v is the number of edges incident on it. The **minimum degree** of G is the minimum of its vertex degrees, let $\Delta(G)$ denote the largest d such that there is an induced subgraph H of G with minimum degree d.

The **vertex connectivity**, written $k(G)$, of an undirected graph G is the minimum number of vertices whose removal results in a disconnected or trivial graph. A graph $G = (V, E)$ is said to be m-**vertex connected** if $k(G) \geq m$. A k-**block** of a graph is a maximal k-edge connected induced subgraph. A **separating set** S of G is a vertex set $S \subseteq V$ such that $G\backslash S$ is disconnected or trivial, where $G\backslash S$ denotes the resulting graph after eliminating the set S of vertices. A **minimum separating set**, $S \subseteq V$, has $|S| = k(G)$.

We are also interested in connectivity through edges. The **edge connectivity**, denoted $\lambda(G)$, of an undirected graph G is the minimum number of edges whose removal results in a disconnected or trivial graph. A graph $G = (V, E)$ is m-**edge connected** if $\lambda(G) \geq m$.

Notice that the three properties are monotone with respect to edge addition, so we have only to show extremal graph results for them, to get approximation algorithms in NC for the corresponding high weight problems; the High Degree Subgraph, the High Vertex Connected Subgraph and the High Edge Connected Subgraph.

Given a graph $G = (V, E)$ with n vertices and m edges, let us start by

considering the case when the property under consideration is the minimum
degree. The following result is a well known result in extremal graph theory
(see for example [ASE92]),

Lemma 3.2.1 (Erdös) *Let G be a graph. Given any $p < n$ such that
$p \cdot n \leq m$, G has an induced subgraph with minimum degree at least p.*

Proof The proof is by induction on the number of vertices. The result holds
trivially for graphs consisting of a single vertex. Suppose that it holds for
any graph with less than n vertices. If G has minimum degree at least p
then we are done. Otherwise, let G' be the graph obtained by deleting a
vertex with smallest degree. Notice that in G' we have $n - 1$ vertices and at
least $m - p$ edges, furthermore unless G is complete p is at most $n - 1$, thus
the statement follows by applying the induction hypothesis to G'.   □

Therefore for the High Degree Subgraph problem, to prove that the prop-
erty is an LEP one, it suffices to take $\sigma = 1$ and $\alpha = \beta = \gamma = 0$ and the
particular case of $p = m/n$. Therefore, the property of minimum degree is
an LEP property, in the sense that G has an induced subgraph which has
minimum degree $\lfloor m/n \rfloor$. By using the procedure FAST we get

Theorem 3.2.2 *The High Degree Subgraph problem can be approximated
in NC, within any ϵ such that $0 < \epsilon < 1/2$.*

Consider now the case when the property W is the edge connectivity of
graphs and assume that a graph $G = (V, E)$ with n vertices and m edges is
given. Before stating the main theorem we will prove a technical lemma,

Lemma 3.2.3 *Let G be a graph such that $n \geq 2$. Then for every p such
that $p \cdot n \leq m + p$, G has an induced p-edge connected subgraph.*

Proof The proof is by induction on the number m of edges. The basis of the
induction is trivial. Assume that the edge connectivity λ of G is less than p.
Let C be a minimum connected set ($|C| = \lambda$). By removing C, the graph G
splits into at least two subgraphs $G_1 = (V_1, E_1)$ and $G_2 = (V_2, E_2)$ such that
$V_1 \cup V_2 = V$, $V_1 \cap V_2 = \emptyset$, $E_1 \cap E_2 = \emptyset$ and $E_1 \cup E_2 \cup C = E$. Let $n_1 = |V_i|$
and $n_2 = |V_2|$, for $i \in \{1, 2\}$. If $pn_1 \leq m_1 + \lambda$ then $pm \leq m_1 + p$ and we are
done. Otherwise $pn_1 > m_1 + \lambda$, hence $m_2 = m - (m_1 + \lambda) > m - pn_1$ so
$m_2 > m - p(n - n_2)$ from which it follows that $pn_2 < m_2 + pn - m \leq m_2 + p$,
therefore by the induction hypothesis G_2 has a p-edge connected subgraph,
thus the lemma follows.   □

Taking in the above lemma the particular case of $p = m/n$ we get that the property of edge connectivity of induced subgraphs is an LEP property, in the sense that G has an induced subgraph which is $\lfloor m/(n-1) \rfloor$-edge connected. Thus by applying the procedure FAST we conclude that the following holds.

Theorem 3.2.4 *The* High Edge Connected Subgraph *problem can be approximated in* NC *within any ϵ such that $0 < \epsilon < 1/2$.*

Let us turn to the case where the property W is the vertex connectivity of graphs. We proceed as we have done before, by proving a technical lemma which will yield the main result. Again $G = (V, E)$ will be a graph with n vertices and m edges.

Lemma 3.2.5 *Let G be a graph. For any $p < n$ such that $p(n-(p+1)/2) \leq m$. Then G has an induced subgraph which is $\lceil (p+1)/2 \rceil$-vertex connected.*

Proof Again we use induction, but this time on the number n of vertices. The basis of the induction is trivial. Suppose now that the lemma is true for graphs with less than n vertices.

If G has a minimum degree less than p, then the statement follows by applying the induction hypothesis to the graph obtained by deleting a vertex of minimum degree. Notice that unless G is complete, in order to apply the induction hypothesis, p cannot be greater than or equal to $n-1$.

Suppose therefore that the minimum degree of G is at least p. In this case, delete from G a minimum separating set S and let $A_1, \ldots, A_r$ for $r \geq 2$ be the resulting components. Let $n_i = |A_i \cup S|$; let m_i be the number of edges with both endpoints in the set $A_i \cup S$; let $n_S = |S|$ and m_S be the number of edges with both points in S. Since G has minimum degree of at least p, then $p < n_i$ for $i \in \{1, \ldots, r\}$, and therefore the induction hypothesis applies on $A_i \cup S$.

Assume that none of the $A_i \cup S$ has a $((p+1)/2)$-vertex connected subgraph, otherwise the statement of the lemma would follow. Then we get that for any $i \in \{1, \ldots, r\}$, $p(n_i - (p+1)/2) > m_i$. Summing up we get

$$p \sum_{i=1}^{r} n_i > \sum_{i=1}^{r} m_i + rp(p+1)/2.$$

But from the definition of n_i and m_i we get that $\sum_{i=1}^{r} n_i = n + (r-1)n_S$ and that $\sum_{i=1}^{r} m_i = m + (r-1)m_S$. Substituting, $pn + p(r-1)m_S > m + (r-1)m_S + rp(p+1)/2$. By the induction hypothesis we know that

$m \geq pn+p(p+1)/2$ so we get $p(r-1)n_S > (r-1)m_S+(r-1)p(p+1)/2$ which is equivalent to $n_S > m_S/p + (p+1)/2 > (p+1)/2$, that is $|S| > (p+1)/2$.

Since the minimum separating set S of G has cardinality greater than $(p+1)/2$, G itself is at least $\lceil (p+1)/2 \rceil$-vertex connected. $\qquad\square$

As in the edge connected case, when we consider the particular case of the lemma with $p = m/n$, we get that the property of vertex connectivity of induced subgraphs is an LEP property, in the sense that G has an induced subgraph which is $\lfloor (m+n)/2n \rfloor$-vertex connected. Again by applying the procedure FAST, we obtain the following result.

Theorem 3.2.6 *The* High Vertex Connected Subgraph *problem is approximable in* NC, *within any ϵ such that $0 < \epsilon < 1/2$.*

4

Rounding, Interval Partitioning and Separation

The approximation techniques that we consider in this chapter apply to problems that can be formulated as *profit/cost* problems, defined as follows: given an $n \times n$ positive matrix C and two positive vectors p and b, find an n-bit vector f such that its cost $C \cdot f$ is bounded by b and its profit $p \cdot f$ is maximized. The value of f is computed incrementally. Starting from the 0 vector, the algorithm analyzes all possible extensions incrementing one bit at a time, until it covers the n bits. Notice that the new set can have twice the size of the previous one thus leading to an exponential size set in the last step. However, we can discard some of the new assignments according to some criteria to get polynomial size sets.

Consider the interval determined by the minimum current profit and the maximum one. In the **interval partitioning** technique this interval is divided into small subintervals. The interval partition also gives a partition of the current set of assignment. From each class the assignment that dominates all others is selected, and the remainder discarded.

In the **separation technique**, the criterion used to discard possible completions insures that there are no duplicated profit values, and the profits of no three partial solutions are within a factor of each other.

The **rounding/scaling** technique is used to deal with problems that are hard due to the presence of large weights in the problem instance. The technique modifies the problem instance in order to produce a second instance that has no large weights, and thus can be solved efficiently. The way in which a new instance is obtained consists in computing first an estimate of the optimal value (when needed) in order to discard unnecessary high weights. Then the weights are modified, scaling them down by an appropriate factor that depends on the estimation and the allowed error. The rounding factor is determined in such a way that the so obtained instance can be solved efficiently. Finally a last step consisting in scaling up the value of the "easy" instance solution is performed in order to meet the corresponding accuracy requirements.

It is known that in the sequential case, the only way to construct FP-TAS uses rounding/scaling and interval partition [KS80]. In general, both techniques can be parallelized, although sometimes the details of the parallelization are non-trivial.   Sahni and Horowitz presented an FPTAS for a variety of sequencing and scheduling problems, among them a whole bunch of Knapsack problems [HS76]. Their techniques are based on interval partitioning. Gens and Levner gave the best known FPTAS for the Subset Sum problem [GL78]. Based on their algorithm Peters and Rudolph gave an FNCAS for this last problem that is easily extensible to other problems known to be in FPTAS [PR87]. For instance, the sequential interval partitioning technique for the 0-1 Knapsack problem can be parallelized to put the problem in FNCAS [Sha75]. The parallel time and work obtained are the same as for the Subset Sum problem. The same remark could be made for Job Sequencing with Deadlines, Minimum m-Processors Scheduling, Minimum m-Processors Scheduling with Speed Factors [PR87].

Goldschlager, Shaw and Staples showed that the Maximum Flow problem is P-complete [GSS82]. The P-completeness proof for Maximum Flow uses large capacities on the edges; in fact the values of some capacities are exponential in the number of network vertices. If the capacities are constrained to be no greater than some polynomial in the number of vertices, we have shown in Section 2.2 that the problem is ZNC. In the case of planar networks it is known that the Maximum Flow problem is in NC, even if arbitrary capacities are allowed [JV87]. The parallel complexity of the Maximum Weight Matching problem when the weight of the edges are given in binary is still an open problem. In Section 2.2 we already shown that there is a randomized NC algorithm to solve the problem in $O(\log^2 n)$ parallel steps, when the weights of the edges are given in unary. The scaling technique has been used to obtain full randomized NC approximation schemes, for the Maximum Flow and Maximum Weight Matching problems ([SS91], [Spi93]). The result appears to be the best possible in regard of full approximation, in the sense that the existence of an FNCAS for any of the problems considered is equivalent to the existence of an NC algorithm for perfect matching. However, as we shall show later the technique can be used, combined with other approximation techniques, to derive NC approximation schemes for both problems.

4.1 The Subset Sum Problem

Let us consider the Subset Sum problem. Let $E = \{1, \ldots, n\}$ be a finite set such that for each $i \in E$ there is an integer size s_i, and given an integer b, the problem asks for a subset $S \subseteq E$ such that $\sum_{i \in S} s_i \leq b$ that maximizes $\sum_{i \in S} s_i$. When $b = \sum_{i=1}^{n} a_i / 2$, the problem is equivalent to the problem of distributing a set of n tasks with known processing times between two known processors in such a way as to minimize the total processing time. Horowitz and Shani presented an FPTAS for the problem, based on interval partitioning [HS76]. Gens and Levner gave the best known FPTAS for the problem [GL78]. Based on their algorithm Peters and Rudolph gave an FNCAS for the Subset Sum problem that is easily extensible to other problems known to be in FPTAS [PR87].

Let us start with an algorithm that provides a $\frac{1}{2}$-approximation to the Subset Sum problem. An instance x is formed by the n weights s_i and the bound b. The scheme is given in Algorithm 10 and can be easily implemented in NC. Furthermore it is easy to verify that the proposed algorithm is a $\frac{1}{2}$-approximation.

APPSSUM(x)
1 Sort $s_1, \ldots, s_n$ into non-increasing order.
2 Compute the n prefix sums of the ordered sequence.
3 Compare the largest sum not exceeding b to a_1.
4 Output the larger of the two values.

Algorithm 10: A $\frac{1}{2}$-NC-approximation to Subset Sum

Lemma 4.1.1 *Algorithm APPSSUM is a $\frac{1}{2}$-NC-approximation to the* Subset Sum *problem. Furthermore it can be implemented in a CREW PRAM to run in $O(\log n)$ time using n processors.*

The Peters and Rudolph scheme is given in Algorithm 11. The algorithm consists in computing recursively a $\frac{1}{2}$-approximation to the actual instance, by a suitable combination of the smallest results a set of partial solutions is constructed. In the last part, the compactification step, some partial solutions are discarded in order to guarantee that the algorithm keeps a bounded number of good partial solutions.

Algorithm 11 can be implemented in parallel using the standard sorting, merging and pointer jumping techniques for PRAM [JaJ92]. Therefore the

---

SSUM(x)

1 $\alpha :=$APPSSUM(x).

2 Recursively solve the problem on $\{s_1, \ldots, s_{n/2}\}$ and $\{s_{n/2+1}, \ldots, s_n\}$. Store the results in arrays (A_1, A_2).

3 For each partial solution $A_1[i]$, generate an array

$$B_i = \{A_1[i] + A_2[j] | A_1[i] + A_2[j] \leq b \text{ for } j = 1, \ldots, n\}.$$

4 Merge the arrays $\{B_i\}$ into one array C by sorting and eliminating duplicates.

5 For each element i for which $C[i]$ is defined, compute the value $N[i]$ such that

$$C[i] + \epsilon\alpha \geq C[k]$$

for $i < k \leq N[i]$.

6 Compact C to obtain an array D following the list with starting point $C[1]$ and using N as pointers.

Algorithm 11: FNCAS for Subset Sum

algorithm can be implemented in NC as long as the arrays used in it have polynomial size. To prove such a bound we need the next lemma, whose proof can be done by a long induction proof on the number of subdivisions, therefore we refer the reader to the original source [PR87].

Lemma 4.1.2 *Let D be the array of partial solutions for an instance x of the* Subset Sum *problem after k parallel divide and conquer steps. Let s be any feasible partial solution of the current subproblem. Then one of the following conditions is true.*

(i) $s \in D$.

(ii) $s \notin D$ *and there are elements $z_1, z_2 \in D$ such that $z_1 < z < z_2$ and $z_2 - z_1 \leq \epsilon\alpha$.*

(iii) $s \notin D$ *and there is an element $z \in D$ such that $z < s < \text{Opt}(x)$ and $\text{Opt}(x) - z < \epsilon\alpha$.*

By using the above lemma we can bound the size of the array D during the execution of Algorithm 11.

Lemma 4.1.3 *The number of elements in the array D is at most $4/\epsilon$ during the whole execution of Algorithm* SSUM.

Proof By Lemma 4.1.2 we have the following conditions: $D[1] = 0$, for all i for which the next element in D is defined $D[i+1] > D[i]$, for all i for which the next but one element in D is defined $D[i+2] - D[i] > \epsilon\alpha$ and finally, for all i it holds that $D[i] \leq \mathrm{Opt}(x) \leq 2\alpha$. Therefore we have

$$|D| \leq \frac{2\mathrm{Opt}(x)}{\epsilon\alpha} \leq \frac{4}{\epsilon}.$$

$\square$

Putting together the above results we obtain the following result.

Theorem 4.1.4 *There is an* FNCAS *to obtain an ϵ-approximate solution to the* Subset Sum *problem in parallel time $O(\log n \log(1/\epsilon))$ and work $W = O(n/\epsilon^2 \times \log n \times \log(1/\epsilon))$ for any $0 < \epsilon < 1$*

As we already mentioned, in a similar way, other known problems in FPTAS have been shown to be also in FNCAS. Gopalakrishnan, Ramakrishnan and Kanal have parallelized directly the scaling technique used by Ibarra and Kim [IK75] for the 0-1 Knapsack problem, to obtain an FNCAS that with respect to the result of Peters and Rudolph reduces by a factor of $(n/\epsilon)^{1/2}$ the number of processors, but also increases the time by a factor of $\log n$ [GRK91].

An interesting open problem is Bin Packing. Karmarkar and Karp have shown that the problem admits an FPTAS$^\infty$ [KK82]. Their algorithm uses the ellipsoid method. It will be interesting to know if the problem belongs to FNCAS$^\infty$. In Chapter 7 we shall devote a section to the parallel approximation for the problem.

4.2 Maximum Flow and Weighted Matching

We use standard definitions for networks and flows (see for example [Law76], [Eve79]). A **network** $N = (G, s, t, c)$ is a structure consisting of a directed graph $G = (V, E)$, two distinguished vertices, $s, t \in V$ (called the **source** and the **sink**), and $c : E \to \mathbb{Z}^+$, an assignment of an integer capacity to each edge in E. A **flow function** f is an assignment of a nonnegative number to each edge of G (called the flow into the edge) such that first at no edge does the flow exceed the capacity, and second for every vertex except s and t, the sum of the flows on its incoming edges equals the sum of the flows on its outgoing edges. The **total flow** of a given flow function

f is defined as the net sum of flow into the sink t. Given a network N, the **Maximum Flow** problem is to find an f for which the total flow is maximum.

Let $G = (V, E)$ be a directed graph, and s, t two vertices. A directed path from s to t, an (s, t)-**path**, is a sequence of edges from s to t. Vertices s and t are said to be **connected** if there exists an (s, t)-path. A subset $C \subseteq E$ is called an (s, t)-**cut set** if in the graph $G' = (V, E - C)$, s and t are disconnected. Note that any (s, t)-cut set C determines a partition of the vertices of the graph into two sets S and T, such that $s \in S$ and $t \in T$ and for which C contains just those edges extending between S and T, conversely every partition S, T, as above, determines an (s, t)-cut set. So we can identify every (s, t)-cut set with a partition S, T. We define the **capacity** of a given cut set $C = (S, T)$ as

$$c(C) = \sum c(e)$$

where the summation extends over all arcs $e = (u, v)$, such that $u \in S$ and $v \in T$.

In the following, given a network $N = (G, s, t, c)$ assume $n = |V|$, $m = |E|$ and $Max(N) = \max_{e \in E}\{c(e)\}$. We now state one of the principal theorems of network flow theory which relates maximum flow with minimum cut, the Max-Flow Min-Cut Theorem [FF62].

Theorem 4.2.1 (Ford, Fulkerson) *The maximum value of a flow is equal to the minimum capacity of an (s, t)-cut.*

Let us study first the relationship between flows and matchings. We will prove that the Maximum Flow problem restricted to networks with polynomial capacities is NC-equivalent to the Maximum Matching problem for bipartite graphs.

In Figure 4.1 is sketched the standard reduction from the Maximum Matching problem for bipartite graphs to the Maximum Flow problem ([Law76], [Pap94]). Dashed lines represent a maximum matching and its corresponding maximum flow. The reverse reduction works in two stages. First assume that the given network N has all edges with capacity one. Then, we construct a bipartite graph that will have as vertex sets two marked copies of the set of edges $V_1 = E \times \{1\}$ and $V_2 = E \times \{2\}$. If $e = (i, j) \in E$ and $u = (j, k) \in E$ then the graph will have edge $((e, 1), (u, 2))$. For every edge $e \in E$ that does not touch the source and the sink, the new graph

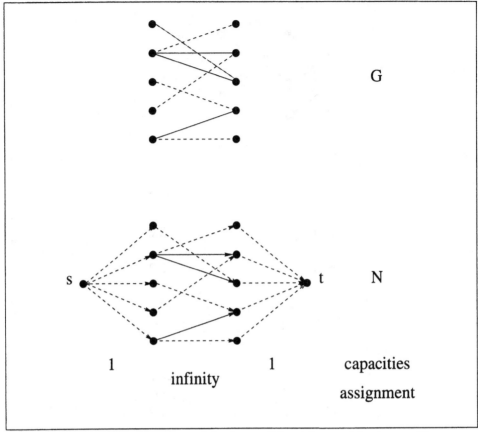

G

N

s   t

1   1   capacities

infinity   assignment

Fig. 4.1: Reduction from Maximum Matching to Maximum Flow

will have edge $((e, 1), (e, 2))$. It is easy to see from Figure 4.2 how we can convert a maximum matching into a maximum flow. In the general case we have just to look at each edge with capacity $c > 1$ as c edges joining the same points each with capacity one, and transform the multigraph obtained as shown before. Notice that to perform this transformation we need a c value polynomially bounded. The whole procedure was introduced by Karp, Upfal and Wigderson [KUW86].

Using the previous transformations we have

Theorem 4.2.2 *The* Maximum Matching *problem for bipartite graphs is* NC *equivalent to the* Maximum Flow *problem on networks with polynomial capacities.*

Notice that the above result places the Maximum Flow with polynomial capacities problem in the class RNC. We can extend this result to a gener-

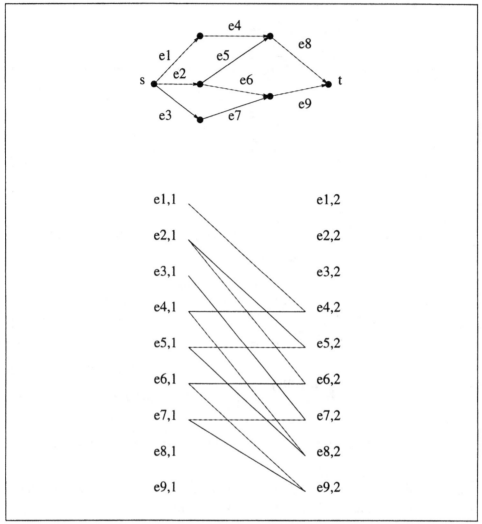

Fig. 4.2: Reduction from Maximum Flow to Maximum Matching

alization of the problem, namely the version Maximum Flow on networks with polynomially bounded maximum flow. The proof is based on the construction (in NC) of a second network which has the same maximum flow but for which the maximum flow and the maximum capacity in the network are polynomially related.

Lemma 4.2.3 *Let* $N = (G, s, t, c)$*. Given any integer* k*, we can decide in NC whether* $f(N) \geq k$ *or* $f(N) < k\,m$*.*

Proof Given k we consider the network $M = (G_1, s, t, c_1)$ defined by

$$G_1 = (V, E_1),$$
$$E_1 = \{e \in E \mid c(e) \geq k\},$$
$$c_1(e) = c(e) \text{ for } e \in E_1.$$

We have to consider two cases:

Case 1: s, t are disconnected in G_1, in this case the original network N must have a minimum (s, t)-cut set C which involves no edge with capacity greater than or equal to k, so we have $c(C) < k|C| \leq km$ and then $f(N) < km$.

Case 2: s, t are connected in G_1, then there is an (s, t)-path P in G formed by edges with capacity greater than or equal to k. Let d be the minimum capacity along the path P, then the flow pattern

$$f(e) = \begin{cases} d & \text{if } e \in P, \\ 0 & \text{otherwise}, \end{cases}$$

is a valid flow pattern for N, thus $f(N) \geq k$.

So an algorithm to decide whether $f(N) \geq k$ or $f(N) < km$ has only to construct the graph G_1 and test whether s and t are connected, and this can be done in NC, provided that the comparisons between $c(e)$ and k (for all e) can be done in NC. These numbers, as inputs to the problem, have to be recognized in NC. Thus, their length (in binary) is at most polynomial. Then the comparisons can be done fast in parallel by partitioning long numbers into consecutive strings of $\lfloor \log n \rfloor$ bits, doing (in parallel) local comparisons and suitably merging the results. □

Since Lemma 4.2.3 applies even to numbers that are exponential in size, we get

Lemma 4.2.4 *Let* $N = (G, s, t, c)$ *be a network. We can compute in NC an integer value* k *such that* $2^k \leq f(N) < m \, 2^{k+1}$.

Proof Let $b = \log(Max(N))$, we can do in parallel the test stated in Lemma 4.2.3 for the values $2^b, 2^{b-1}, \ldots, 2^0$. As $f(N)$ is at least zero and at most $m \, 2^b$, there will be a unique k for which s, t are connected through edges with capacity at least 2^k and disconnected through edges with capacity at least 2^{k+1}. In this case we have $f(N) \geq 2^k$ and $f(N) < 2^{k+1}m$. Note that the values $2^b, 2^{b-1}, \ldots, 2^0$ are $b+1$, that means $\log(Max(N)) + 1$, and therefore at most a polynomial in the input size. □

The following lemma establishes the NC-reduction from the Maximum Flow problem with polynomial maximum flow to the Maximum Flow problem with polynomial capacities.

Lemma 4.2.5 *Let $N = (G, s, t, c)$ be a network, we can construct in NC a second network $N_1 = (G, s, t, c_1)$ such that*

$$\log(Max(N_1)) \leq \log(f(N_1)) + O(\log n)$$

and $f(N) = f(N_1)$.

Proof Let k be the value obtained in Lemma 4.2.4, to define N_1 we only change the capacity assignment of G as follows:

$$c_1(e) = \begin{cases} 2^{k+1}m & \text{if } c(e) \geq 2^{k+1}m, \\ c(e) & \text{otherwise.} \end{cases}$$

Trivially, N_1 has the same minimum cuts as N, just note that no edge with capacity greater than $2^{k+1}m$ can be in a minimum cut for N, hence, $f(N_1) = f(N)$. By Lemma 4.2.4 we then have $2^k \leq f(N_1) < 2^{k+1}m$ and $Max(N_1) \leq 2^{k+1}m$ i.e., $Max(N_1) \leq 2mf(N_1)$. $\qquad\square$

Lemma 4.2.5 shows that the Maximum Flow problem restricted to networks with polynomially bounded maximum flow is NC-reducible to the Maximum Flow problem restricted to polynomially bounded capacities, the latter problem is a simplification of the former one, so we have

Theorem 4.2.6 *For each polynomial p, the problem of constructing a maximum flow in a network N such that $f(N) \leq p(n)$ is NC-equivalent to the problem of constructing a maximum matching in a bipartite graph, and thus it is in RNC.*

Recall that Algorithm 7 gave us an $O(\log^2 n)$ parallel time to compute a maximum matching. Combining the reduction from the Maximum Flow problem to the Maximum Matching problem given in Figure 4.2 with Algorithm 7 we otain the following result.

Theorem 4.2.7 *There is a randomized parallel algorithm to construct a maximum flow in a directed network, such that the number of processors is bounded by a polynomial in the number of vertices and the time used is $O((\log n)^\alpha \log f(N))$ for some constant $\alpha > 0$.*

4.3 Approximating Maximum Flow

We show here that the general problem of finding a maximum flow in a network N can be approximated by an RNC algorithm which, given N and an $\epsilon > 0$, outputs a solution f' such that $f(N)/f' \leq 1 + 1/\epsilon$. The algorithm uses a polynomial number of processors (independent of ϵ) and parallel time $O(\log^\alpha n(\log n + \log \epsilon))$, where α is independent of ϵ. Thus the algorithm is an RNC one as long as ϵ is at most polynomial in n. (Actually ϵ can be $O(n^{\log^\beta n})$ for some β.)

Let us start by giving a rough NC approximation to the Maximum Flow problem.

Lemma 4.3.1 *Let $N = (G, s, t, c)$ be a network. Let $k \geq 1$ be an integer, then there is an NC algorithm to construct a network $M = (G, s, t, c_1)$ such that $k \, f(M) \leq f(N) \leq k \, f(M) + km$.*

Proof We consider the network M defined by

$$c_1(e) = \left\lfloor \frac{c(e)}{k} \right\rfloor \qquad \text{for all } e \in E.$$

Then for a given (s, t)-cut set C the following hold:

$$c(C) \leq k c_1(C) + k|C|; \tag{4.1}$$
$$k c_1(C) \leq c(C). \tag{4.2}$$

Let A be a min cut for N and B a min cut for M, therefore $c(A) = f(N)$ and $c_1(B) = f(M)$. We have:

- As B is a min cut for M, $c_1(B) \leq c_1(A)$, and then $k c_1(B) \leq k c_1(A)$.
- Using (4.2) we have $k c_1(A) \leq c(A)$.
- As A is a min cut for N, $c(A) \leq c(B)$.
- Using (4.1) we have $c(B) \leq k c_1(B) + k|B| \leq k c_1(B) + km$.

So we conclude that $k c_1(B) \leq c(A) \leq k c_1(B) + km$; therefore $k f(M) \leq f(N) \leq k f(M) + km$. $\qquad \square$

The previous result can be improved by allowing randomization.

Theorem 4.3.2 *Let $N = (G, s, t, c)$ be a network. Then, there is an RNC algorithm such that for all $\epsilon > 0$ at most polynomial in the number of network vertices, the algorithm computes a legal flow of value f' such that*

$$\frac{f(N)}{f'} \leq 1 + \frac{1}{\epsilon}.$$

Furthermore, the algorithm uses a polynomial number of processors and runs in expected parallel time $O(\log^\alpha n(\log n + \log \epsilon))$, for some constant α, independent of ϵ.

Proof Algorithm 12 satisfies the theorem:

FAST-FLOW(N, ϵ)
Let $N = (G, s, t, c)$.
1 Compute k such that $2^k \leq F(N) \leq 2^{k+1}m$.
2 Construct a network N_1 such that

$$\log(Max(N_1)) \leq \log(F(N_1)) + O(\log n).$$

3 If $2^k \leq (1+\epsilon)m$ then $F(N) \leq (1+\epsilon)m^2$ so use Algorithm 7 to solve the Maximum Flow problem in N as a Maximum Matching and **return**
4 Let $\beta = \left\lfloor \dfrac{2^k}{(1+\epsilon)m} \right\rfloor$. Construct N_2 from N_1 and β using the construction in Lemma 4.3.1.
5 Use Algorithm 7 to solve the Maximum Flow problem in N_2 as a Maximum Matching.
6 Output $F' = \beta F(M_2)$ and for all $e \in E$, $f'(e) = \beta f(e)$.

Algorithm 12: FRNCAS for Max Flow

Notice in step 1 we use Lemma 4.2.4. In step 2, we use Lemma 4.2.5. In step 4, $\beta \geq 1$ is an integer. Moreover it can be constructed in NC, and

$$F(N_2) \leq F(N)/\beta \leq \frac{2^{k+1}m}{\beta} = O(\epsilon m^2);$$

thus N_2 has polynomially bounded maximum flow. Finally, the procedure in step 5 is a RNC algorithm.

It is not too difficult to prove that the processors and parallel time as well as the approximation ratio are the ones in the statment of the theorem.
Claim 1: The processors and parallel time of FAST-FLOW satisfy the theorem.

Proof Steps 1, 2, 4 and 6 can be done in NC, independently of the actual value of ϵ. In steps 3 and 5 the call to the Maximum Matching algorithm uses a polynomial (in n) number of processors and expected parallel time $O(\log^\alpha n \log F(N))$ for some $\alpha > 1$, independent of ϵ, i.e., parallel time $(\log^\alpha n (\log n + \log \epsilon))$. □

Claim 2: The approximation ratio R FAST-FLOW(N, ϵ) is less than or equal to $1 + 1/\epsilon$.

Proof By definition of approximation ratio,

$$R \text{ FAST-FLOW}(N, \epsilon) = \frac{F(N)}{F'} = \frac{F(N)}{\beta F(N_2)}.$$

But, as we have shown in Lemma 4.3.1, $F(N) \le \beta F(N_2) + \beta m$. Thus,

$$R \text{ FAST-FLOW}(N, \epsilon) \le 1 + \frac{\beta m}{\beta F(N_2)}.$$

Since $\beta F(N_2) \ge F(N) - \beta m$ and $F(N) \ge 2^k$ we get $\beta F(N_2) \ge 2^k - \beta m$, therefore we get

$$R \text{ FAST-FLOW}(N, \epsilon) \le 1 + \frac{\beta m}{2^k - \beta m}.$$

As we know, $\beta \le \dfrac{2^k}{(1+\epsilon)m}$ and $2^k - \beta m \ge 2^k - \dfrac{2^k}{1+\epsilon} = \dfrac{\epsilon 2^k}{1+\epsilon}$, hence,

$$\frac{\beta m}{2^k - \beta m} \le 1/\epsilon$$

and thus, R FAST-FLOW$(N, \epsilon) \le 1 + 1/\epsilon$, and Claim 2 follows. □

This completes the proof of Theorem 4.3.2. □

4.4 Approximating Maximum Weight Matching

Now we consider the weighted version of the Maximum Matching problem. Given a graph $G = (V, E)$ and a weight $w(e)$ for each edge $e \in E$, the Maximum Weight Matching problem asks for a matching of G with the largest possible sum of weights.

To reduce the Maximum Weight Matching problem to the Maximum Weight Perfect Matching problem, we can assume that the graph is always complete by letting the weights of those edges that were missing be zero. Furthermore, we can also assume that G has an even number of vertices, otherwise add a new vertex with edges of weight zero incident upon it. Therefore, the maximum weight matching coincides with the maximum weight perfect matching. In the Maximum Weight Matching problem, the weight of a matching is polynomially bounded only when the edge weights are polynomially bounded. Thus we show directly that the Maximum Weight Matching problem with weights given in binary can be approximated by an RNC algorithm which, given a weighted graph G and an $\epsilon > 0$, outputs a solution M' such that $M(G)/M' \leq 1 + 1/\epsilon$. The algorithm uses a polynomial (in n and ϵ) number of processors and parallel time $O(\log^2 n)$. Thus as long as ϵ is at most polynomial in n, the algorithm is an RNC one.

Lemma 4.4.1 *Let $G = (V, E)$ be a graph with edge weights given in binary. Let $k \geq 1$ be an integer, then we can construct in NC a weighted graph $G' = (V, E)$ such that $k\, M(G') \leq M(G) \leq k\, M(G') + kn/2$, where n denotes the number of vertices in G.*

Proof We consider the graph G' with weights defined by

$$w'(e) = \left\lfloor \frac{w(e)}{k} \right\rfloor \qquad \text{for all } e \in E.$$

Let X' be a maximum weight perfect matching in G'; as X' is also a maximum weight perfect matching in G, we get

$$k\, M(G') \leq k\, w'(X') \leq w(X') \leq M(G).$$

Let X be a maximum weight perfect matching in G. We have

$$w(X) = \sum_{\substack{e \in X \\ w(e) \geq k}} w(e) + \sum_{\substack{e \in X \\ w(e) < k}} w(e)$$

$$\leq \sum_{\substack{e \in X \\ w(e) \geq k}} k\left(\left\lfloor \frac{w(e)}{k} \right\rfloor + 1 \right) + \sum_{\substack{e \in X \\ w(e) < k}} w(e)$$

$$\leq w'(X) + k|X| \leq k\, M(G') + k\frac{n}{2}.$$

So the lemma holds.   □

Theorem 4.4.2 *Let $G = (V, E)$ be a weighted graph. Then, there is an RNC algorithm such that for all $\epsilon > 0$ at most polynomial in the number of network vertices, the algorithm computes a perfect matching of weight M' such that*

$$\frac{M(G)}{M'} \leq 1 + \frac{1}{\epsilon}.$$

Furthermore, the algorithm uses $O(n^{5.5} m^2 \epsilon)$ processors and runs in expected parallel time $O(\log^2 n)$.

Proof Let W be the weight of the heaviest edge in G. Then Algorithm 13 satisfies the theorem.

FAST-MATCHING(G, ϵ)
Given a weighted graph $G = (V, E)$.
1 Compute $k = \lfloor \log W \rfloor$.
2 If $2^k \leq (1+\epsilon)n$ then use Algorithm 7 to find the Maximum Weight Perfect Matching and **return**.
3 Let $\beta = \left\lfloor \dfrac{2^k}{(1+\epsilon)n} \right\rfloor$.
   Construct G' from G and β using the construction of Lemma 4.4.1.
4 Solve the Maximum Matching problem in G' using Algorithm 7.
5 **Return** $M' = \beta M(G')$ and X'.

Algorithm 13: FRNCAS for Max Weight Matching

Notice, in step 1 of the algorithm, we have $2^k \leq F(N) \leq 2^k n$. In step 2, if the If condition is satisfied, we must have $W \leq (1 + \epsilon)n^2$, therefore Algorithm 7 can be applied. In step 3, $\beta \geq 1$ is an integer. Moreover, the β value can be constructed in NC, and therefore we have $W' \leq 2^k n / \beta = O(\epsilon n^2)$, thus G' has polynomially bounded edge weights.

Let us see that the algorithm satisfies the performance bounds of the theorem. The time and processor bounds follow as in the previous section. Using the same argument as in Claim 2 of Theorem 4.3.2, we have that the approximation ratio $R_{\text{FAST-MATCHING}}(G, \epsilon) \leq 1 + 1/\epsilon$. $\qquad \square$

4.5 NC Approximations to Flows and Matchings

Using the second part of the algorithm in Lemma 4.2.4, the condition in step 1 of the FAST-MATCHING algorithm (Algorithm 13), and the reduction from maximum weight matching to maximum weight perfect matching, we have

Lemma 4.5.1 *The following properties hold.*

(i) *There is an NC approximation algorithm $\mathcal{A}$ for the Maximum Flow problem such that $R_{\mathcal{A}} = 2m$ where m is the number of edges.*

(ii) *There is an* NC *approximation algorithm* $\mathcal{A}$ *for the* Maximum Weight Perfect Matching *problem such that* $R_{\mathcal{A}} = n$ *where* n *is the number of vertices.*

(iii) *There is an* NC *approximation algorithm* $\mathcal{A}$ *for the* Maximum Weight Matching *problem such that* $R_{\mathcal{A}} = n.$

Thus the results obtained in the previous sections give us

Theorem 4.5.2 *The following properties hold.*

(i) *There exists a full* RNC *approximation scheme for the* Maximum Flow *problem, with a parallel time bound of* $O(\log n)$.

(ii) *There exists a full* RNC *approximation scheme for the* Maximum Weight Perfect Matching *problem, with a parallel time bound of* $O(\log^2 n)$.

(iii) *There is a full* RNC *approximation scheme for the* Maximum Weight Matching *problem, with a parallel time bound of* $O(\log^2 n)$.

Using the fact that when a problem Π is solvable by a pseudo-NC algorithm, the subproblem obtained by restricting Π to only those instances which involve polynomially bounded numbers is solvable in NC, Lemma 2.7.2, and that the Maximum Flow problem satisfies these conditions, we conclude that the following holds.

Theorem 4.5.3 *There exists a full* NC *approximation scheme for finding a maximum flow, a maximum weight perfect matching and a maximum weight matching if and only if there exists an* NC *algorithm to construct a maximum matching in a graph.*

All the above proofs have been done resorting to Monte Carlo algorithms. Making use of the algorithm developed by Karloff, the Monte Carlo approximations can be transformed into Las Vegas approximations, thus the above results could be stated in terms of ZNC [Kar86].

Cohen has shown that there is an NCAS for the Maximum Flow problem on acyclic networks with constant depth, where the depth of the acyclic network is defined as the length of the longest path between s and t [Coh92].

Another interesting result deals with the NC approximability of the Perfect Matching problems for graphs with weights satisfying the triangle inequality. Ravindran, Holloway and Gibbons proved that the Maximum Weight Matching problem can be approximated in NC by a factor of $2\log_3 n$ for weighted graphs that satisfy the triangle inequality [RHG93].

5

Primal–Dual Method

The linear programming primal–dual method has been extensively used to obtain sequential exact algorithms (see for example [Chv79], [PS82]). This algorithm keeps both a primal solution and a dual solution. When the solutions together satisfy the *complementary slackness* conditions, then they are mutually optimal. Otherwise either the primal solution is augmented or the dual solution is improved. The primal–dual method was originally due to Dantzing, Ford and Fulkerson [DFF56]. Unless P=NP, the primal–dual method cannot be used to solve exactly in polynomial time NP-hard problems.

The primal–dual framework has been particularly useful to obtain polynomial time approximation algorithms for some NP-hard combinatorial optimization problems (see for example the forthcoming survey by Goemans and Williamson [GW96]). For those problems that can be formulated as integer programming problems, the approach works with the linear programming relaxation and its dual, and seeks for an integral extension of the linear programming solution. Furthermore the use of the combinatorial structure of each problem determines how to design the improvement steps and how to carry on the proof of approximation guarantee. There is no general primal–dual approximate technique; however, some approaches can be seen as producing both primal and dual feasible solutions, until some conditions are met. Those last conditions insure that the values of the primal and dual solutions are within $1 + \epsilon$ of each other. As the optima of the primal and dual problems are the same, the primal and dual feasible solutions produced by the algorithm have a value within $1 + \epsilon$ of optimal value.

In the parallel setting there is no hope of parallelizing the primal–dual technique for general linear programming problems. Serna has shown that the general linear programming problem cannot be approximated in NC

[Ser91] (see also Chapter 8). Luby and Nisan [LN93] gave an NC approximation scheme for the positive linear programming problem, thus providing a general framework to approximate all combinatorial problems that can be reduced to a positive linear program, like the Maximum Matching or the Set Cover problems. We can further use the results of Luby and Nisan combined with our previous scheme to obtain NC approximation schemes for the Maximum Flow and the Maximum Weight Matching problems.

Some other primal–dual approximation algorithms are obtained as parallel versions of the corresponding polynomial time approximation algorithm. For example for the Set Cover problem: Berger, Rompel and Shor gave the first (R)NC approximation algorithm for the problem [BRS89]. The techniques of Luby and Nisan also apply because the linear programming relaxation is a positive problem. Khuller, Vishkin and Young [KVY93] present an NC approximation algorithm for the Weighted Vertex Cover problem that is a parallelization of the algorithm of Hochbaum [Hoc82]. Rajagopalan and Vazirani [RV89] give an RNC approximation algorithm for the set cover and its extensions, their algorithm is based on the classical greedy algorithm.

5.1 Positive Linear Programming

Let us begin by considering the primal and dual formulations of the linear programming problem. The primal linear programming problem consists in finding a rational vector $z = (z_1, \ldots, z_n)$ that minimizes $\sum_{i=1}^{n} z_i$ subject to the constraints:

- For all i, $z_i \geq 0$
- For all j, $\sum_{i} a_{i,j} z_i \geq 1$

Notice that an easy transformation allows the restatement of any linear programming problem in this form with integer coefficients (see for example [PS82]).

The dual linear programming problem is to compute a rational vector $u = (u_1, \ldots, u_n)$ that maximizes $\sum_{i=1}^{n} u_i$ subject to the constraints:

- For all j, $u_j \geq 0$
- For all i, $\sum_{j} a_{i,j} u_j \leq 1$

We say that a linear programming problem is **positive** when all the coefficients involved are nonnegative. Notice that not all linear programming problems can be formulated with this restriction, in general we get integer coefficients instead of positive. Furthermore, the method only applies for inequalities.

We can further make restrictions on the size of the coefficients: given $\gamma > 0$, we say that a positive linear programming problem is in γ-**form** if $1 \geq a_{i,j} \geq 1/\gamma$, for all i, j. It is well known how to transform any positive linear program into a γ-form, but at the cost of losing a factor of the optimal solution [LN93].

Lemma 5.1.1 (Luby, Nisan) *Given $\epsilon > 0$, any positive linear programming problem Π can be reduced to a γ-form positive linear programming problem Π' with $\gamma = m^2/\epsilon^2$, and the optima of both problems satisfy $Opt(\Pi) \leq Opt(\Pi') \leq (1+\epsilon)Opt(\Pi)$*

Let us describe now the Luby–Nisan algorithm to compute an approximation to a γ-form positive linear programming problem. The computation is driven by a vector $\mathbf{x} = (x_1, \ldots, x_n)$ whose values change at each step.

From $\mathbf{x}$ the remaining parameters are computed as follows:

$$
\begin{aligned}
\mathbf{x} &= (x_1, \ldots, x_n), & \mathbf{y} &= (y_1, \ldots, y_m), \\
A_j &= \textstyle\sum_i a_{i,j} x_i, & y_j &= e^{-A_j}, \\
A &= \min A_j, & D_i &= \textstyle\sum_j a_{i,j} y_j, \\
\mathbf{z} &= \mathbf{x}/A, & D &= \max D_i, \\
& & \mathbf{u} &= \mathbf{y}/D.
\end{aligned}
$$

The initial $\mathbf{x}$ is the zero vector. Notice that except when $A = 0$ (and this will happen only at the initial step), we have

$$
\begin{aligned}
\textstyle\sum_i a_{i,j} x_i &\geq A, & \textstyle\sum_j a_{i,j} y_j &\leq D, \\
\textstyle\sum_i a_{i,j} z_i &\geq 1, & \textstyle\sum_j a_{i,j} u_j &\leq 1.
\end{aligned}
$$

Thus $\mathbf{z}$ is primal feasible and $\mathbf{u}$ is dual feasible.

For sake of simplicity we specify only the actual value of x, therefore any reference to the other variables obtained from x in Algorithm 14 should be derived according to the actual value of x. The algorithm works in phases, so that at the end of phase k the corresponding D value satisfies

$$(1+\delta)^k \leq D \leq (1+\delta)^{k+1}.$$

Phase indices move in decreasing order, thus during a phase the D value is decremented by a factor of $(1+\delta)$, for some $\delta > 0$.

$\quad$ PLP $([a_{ij}], \delta)$

1 $\quad$ $\mathbf{x} := \mathbf{0}$; $\mathbf{uf} := \mathbf{u}$;

2 $\quad$ Compute k, the smallest positive integer such that
$\quad$ $(1 + \delta)^k < D \le (1 + \delta)^{k+1}$;

3 $\quad$ **while** sum($\mathbf{y}$) $\le 1/m^{1/\delta}$ **do**

4 $\qquad$ **repeat**

5 $\qquad\quad$ $B := \{i | D_i \ge (1 + \delta)^k\}$;

6 $\qquad\quad$ **if** $B = \emptyset$ **then return**;

5 $\qquad\quad$ $\lambda_0 :=$ SPLIT($[a_{ij}], B, x$);

6 $\qquad\quad$ **for all** $i \in B$, $x_i := x_i + \lambda_0$ **do**

7 $\qquad\quad$ **if** sum($\mathbf{u}$) $\ge$ sum($\mathbf{uf}$)

8 $\qquad\qquad$ **then uf** $:= \mathbf{u}$;

9 $\qquad$ **until** $D \le (1 + \delta)^k$;

10 $\qquad$ Compute k, the smallest positive integer such that
$\qquad$ $(1 + \delta)^k < D \le (1 + \delta)^{k+1}$;

11 **Return z and uf**

Algorithm 14: NCAS for Positive Linear Programming

We shall use the following notation. $[k] = \{1, \ldots, k\}$. For any $\lambda \ge 0$ and $B \in [n]$, let

$$S_+(\lambda) = \{j : \lambda \sum_{i \in B} a_{i,j} \ge \delta\}, \qquad D_i^+(\lambda) = \sum_{j \in S_+(\lambda)} a_{i,j} y_j,$$
$$S_-(\lambda) = \{j : \lambda \sum_{i \in B} a_{i,j} \le \delta\}, \qquad D_i^-(\lambda) = \sum_{j \in S_-(\lambda)} a_{i,j} y_j;$$

also for the sake of simplicity for any vector $\mathbf{x}$, sum($\mathbf{x}$) will represent the sum of its components. The main iteration step consists in finding a value λ such that adding this value to the x components in the set B of step 5, at least a fraction $1 - \delta$ of the $i \in B$ satisfy $D_i^-(\lambda_0) \ge (1 - \delta)D_i$. And at least a fraction δ of the $i \in B$ satisfy $D_i^+(\lambda_0) \ge \delta D_i$. Algorithm 15 computes the value of λ_0.

The correctness of Algorithm 14 follows from the following lemma; its proof is easy and it is left as an exercise.

Lemma 5.1.2 *The λ_0 value computed by the* SPLIT *algorithm satisfies:*

(i) *For at least a fraction $1 - \delta$ of the $i \in B$, $D_i^-(\lambda_0) \ge (1 - \delta)D_i$.*

(ii) *For at least a fraction δ of the $i \in B$, $D_i^+(\lambda_0) \ge \delta D_i$.*

SPLIT(A, B, x)

1 For each j, $1 < j < m$, compute $\phi_j := \delta / \sum_{i \in B} a_{i,j}$.

2 Sort the set $\{(\phi_j, j) \mid 1 < j < m\}$ in decreasing order,
   to obtain a permutation π that satisfies $\phi_{\pi(1)} \geq \cdots \geq \phi_{\pi(m)}$.

3 For each $j \in m$ compute j^-, the smallest index, and
   j^+, the largest index for which $\phi_{\pi(j^-)} = \phi_{\pi(j)} = \phi_{\pi(j^+)}$.

4 For each $i \in B$ and $1 \leq j \leq m$ compute
   $D_i^-(\phi_{\pi(j)}) = \sum_{k \leq j^+} a_{i,\pi(j)} \, y_{\pi(j)}$,
   $D_i^+(\phi_{\pi(j)}) = \sum_{k \geq j^-} a_{i,\pi(j)} \, y_{\pi(j)}$.

5 For each $i \in B$ compute an index $v(i)$ such that
   $D_i^-(\phi_{\pi(v(i))}) \geq (1 - \delta) D_i$,
   $D_i^+(\phi_{\pi(v(i))}) \geq \delta D_i$.

6 Find an ordering $b_1, \ldots, b_{|B|}$ of B that satisfies
   $\phi_{\pi(v(b_1))} \geq \cdots \geq \phi_{\pi(v(b_{|B|}))}$.

7 Compute i_0 so that $\frac{i_0}{|B|} \geq (1 - \delta)$ and $\frac{|B| - i_0 + 1}{|B|} \geq \delta$.

8 Return $\phi_{\pi(v(b_{i_0}))}$.

Algorithm 15: Computing the splitting value for PLP

To analyze the complexity of the algorithm let us begin by bounding the total number of phases in Algorithm 14.

Lemma 5.1.3 *The total number of phases is at most* $O\left(\frac{\log(m/\delta)}{\delta^2} \right)$.

Proof Recall that the positive linear programming instance is given in γ-form, so we have $1/\gamma \leq a_{i,j} \leq 1$ and thus

$$\frac{\text{sum}(\mathbf{y})}{\gamma} \leq \sum_j a_{i,j} \, y_j = D_j \leq \text{sum}(\mathbf{y}),$$

the inequality also holds for D, the maximum of the D_i values.

Thus, when all $y_j = 1$, just at the beginning of the algorithm, we get $D \leq m$, and taking $k = O(\log m/\delta)$, D is at most $(1 + \delta)^{k+1}$. When $D \leq \frac{1}{\gamma m^{1/\delta}}$,

$$\text{sum}(\mathbf{y}) \leq \gamma D \leq \frac{1}{m^{1/\delta}},$$

algorithm PLP terminates. Therefore, it never reaches a phase k for which $(1 + \delta)^k \leq \frac{1}{\gamma m^{1/\delta}}$, so that the last phase occurs before phase k_f where

$$k_f = O\left(\frac{\log(m/\delta)}{\delta^2}\right).$$

Therefore the total number of phases is at most $O\left(\frac{\log(m/\delta)}{\delta^2}\right)$.   □

The number of iterations per phase comes from the number of calls to the SPLIT routine before the obtained value fulfills the condition of step 9 in Algorithm 14.

Lemma 5.1.4 *The number of iterations during phase k is at most $O(\frac{\log n}{\delta^2})$.*

Proof At least a fraction δ of the $i \in B$ have $D_i^+(\lambda_0) \geq \delta D_i$. Further, for each $j \in S_+(\lambda_0)$, y_j goes down by at least a factor of $\exp(-\delta) \approx 1 - \delta$. Thus at the end of an iteration a fraction of at least δ of the D_i for $i \in B$ go down by at least a factor $1 - \delta^2$.

But when any of the D_i goes down by a factor of at least $1 - \delta$ the index i is removed from B. That means that the number of iterations is bounded by the logarithm of the initial size of B divided by δ^2. Taking into account that the number of indices $i \in B$ is at most n we get the desired bound.   □

The above lemmas give us the bound on the number of iterations in Algorithm 14,

Lemma 5.1.5 *The total number of iterations is at most*

$$O\left(\log(n) \times \log(m/\delta)/\delta^4\right).$$

To evaluate the parallel use of resources, we use the known parallel algorithms for sorting and prefix sum, which the reader can find in any standard book on parallel algorithms.

Lemma 5.1.6 *Each iteration can be performed in parallel using $O(|A|)$ processors in time $O(\log|A|)$ on an EREW PRAM.*

Proof The most costly part of the algorithm is the computation of SPLIT. But it consists of a constant number of parallel prefix, sort and binary search operations. Using the classical parallel prefix algorithm each iteration can be executed using $O(|A|)$ processors in time $O(\log|A|)$ on an EREW PRAM.   □

Therefore we can bound the total costs of the algorithm for any given value of δ.

Lemma 5.1.7 *Given $\delta > 0$, Algorithm PLP takes $O(\frac{\log n}{\delta^4})$ time using $|A|$ processors.*

To show the optimality of the algorithm, let us first bound the decrement in the sum of the $\mathbf{y}$ vector after one iteration within a phase. Recall that $y_j = -\exp(A_j)$, assume that λ_0 is the increased value of the $\mathbf{x}$ components in a subset index B, and let $\mathbf{y}'$ represent the so obtained vector. Then we have

Lemma 5.1.8 $\operatorname{sum}(\mathbf{y}') \leq \operatorname{sum}(\mathbf{y}) - \lambda_0 D |B| (1 - 4\delta)$.

Proof Notice that

$$\operatorname{sum}(\mathbf{y}') - \operatorname{sum}(\mathbf{y}) = \sum_j y_j \left(1 - \exp\left(-\lambda_0 \sum_{i \in B} a_{i,j} \right) \right).$$

Furthermore observe that for any $\beta \leq 1$, it holds that $1 - \exp(\beta) \geq \beta(1 - \beta)$. Letting $\beta = \lambda_0 \sum_{i \in B} a_{i,j}$ when $j \in S_-(\lambda_0)$ we have that $\beta \leq \delta$. Thus in such a case we have $1 - \exp(\beta) \geq \beta(1 - \delta)$ and that means for all $j \in S_-(\lambda_0)$

$$1 - \exp\left(-\lambda_0 \sum_{i \in B} a_{i,j} \right) \geq \lambda_0 \sum_{i \in B} a_{i,j}(1 - \delta).$$

Putting all this together we get

$$\begin{aligned}
\operatorname{sum}(\mathbf{y}') - \operatorname{sum}(\mathbf{y}) &\geq \textstyle\sum_{j \in S_-(\lambda_0)} (y'_j - y_j) \\
&\geq \textstyle\sum_{j \in S_-(\lambda_0)} y_j \left(1 - \exp\left(-\lambda_0 \sum_{i \in B} a_{i,j} \right) \right) \\
&\geq \textstyle\sum_{j \in S_-(\lambda_0), i \in B} a_{i,j} y_j \lambda_0 (1 - \delta) \\
&= \textstyle\sum_{i \in B} D_i^-(\lambda_0).
\end{aligned}$$

For at least a fraction $(1-\delta)$ of the $i \in B$ we have that $D_i^-(\lambda_0) \geq (1-\delta)D_i$, and since $D_i \geq D/(1 + \delta)$ it follows that the last sum is at least

$$\frac{(1 - \delta)(1 - \delta)D|B|}{1 + \delta}.$$

Thus

$$\operatorname{sum}(\mathbf{y}') - \operatorname{sum}(\mathbf{y}) \geq \lambda_0 D |B| (1 - 4\delta).$$

$\square$

For the sake of simplicity let $\theta = 4\delta$, then we have

Lemma 5.1.9 *The value of* sum(x) *is bounded above by*

$$\frac{\text{sum}(\mathbf{u}) \ln(m/\text{sum}(\mathbf{y}))}{1 - \theta}.$$

Proof From the previous lemma we have that

$$\frac{\text{sum}(\mathbf{y}')}{\text{sum}(\mathbf{y})} \leq 1 - \frac{\lambda_0 D\,|B|\,(1-\theta)}{\text{sum}(\mathbf{y})}$$
$$\leq \exp\left(-\frac{\lambda_0\,|B|\,(1-\theta)}{\text{sum}(\mathbf{y})/D}\right)$$
$$\leq \exp\left(-\frac{\lambda_0\,|B|\,(1-\theta)}{\text{sum}(\mathbf{u})}\right).$$

Taking into account that sum($\mathbf{y}$) $\leq m$ through the whole process, and that the total increase of sum($\mathbf{x}$) in one iteration is $\lambda_0|B|$, it follows that at any step

$$\text{sum}(\mathbf{y}) \leq m \exp\left(\frac{-(1-\theta)\text{sum}(\mathbf{x})}{\text{sum}(\mathbf{u})}\right)$$

and this implies the desired result. $\qquad\qquad\Box$

Taking $\epsilon = 5\delta$, we get the accuracy of the solution computed by Algorithm 14.

Lemma 5.1.10 *Both* sum($\mathbf{z}^*$) *and* sum($\mathbf{u}^*$), *are within a* $1 + \epsilon$ *factor of the optimal solution.*

Proof From the previous lemma and the definition of $\mathbf{z}^*$ it follows that

$$\text{sum}(\mathbf{z}^*) \leq \frac{\text{sum}(\mathbf{u}^*) \ln(m/\text{sum}(\mathbf{y}^*))}{A^*(1 - \theta)}.$$

Since $\ln(m/\text{sum}(\mathbf{y}^*)) \leq A^*$ it follows that

$$\text{sum}(\mathbf{z}^*) \leq \text{sum}(\mathbf{u}^*)(1 + \theta)\frac{\ln(m/\text{sum}(\mathbf{y}^*))}{\ln(1/\text{sum}(\mathbf{y}^*))}.$$

Since at the end of the algorithm

$$\text{sum}(\mathbf{y}^*) \leq \frac{1}{m^{1/\delta}}$$

the primal and dual solutions are within $1 + 5\delta$. Take into account that the optimal value is in between any primal–dual feasible pair, and the result follows. $\qquad\qquad\Box$

Algorithm 14 can be used to deal with positive linear programs. First transform the problem instance into an adequate γ-form so that the overall approximative factor becomes $1 + \epsilon$. Thus the overall time of the algorithm is polynomial in $\frac{\log n}{\epsilon}$ using a polynomial in n number of processors.

Theorem 5.1.11 (Luby, Nisan) *The* positive linear programming *problem is in the class* NCAS.

5.2 Further Applications

The Maximum Matching problem for bipartite graphs can be formulated as the following linear program:

$$\begin{cases} \max \sum_{ij} x_{ij}, \\ \sum_j x_{ij} \leq 1 \text{ for } i = 1, \dots, n, \\ \sum_i x_{ij} \leq 1 \text{ for } j = 1, \dots, n, \\ x_{ij} \geq 0 \text{ for } 1 \leq i, j \leq n, \end{cases}$$

that is the dual of a positive program. Therefore the previous algorithm can be used to approximate the value of a maximum matching for the graph, although it does not provide the matching itself, combined with the techniques in [Coh92] an approximate matching can be obtained, thus we have the following.

Theorem 5.2.1 (Luby, Nisan) *The problem of* Maximum Matching *is in the class* NCAS.

Recall the FRNCAS given in the previous section for the Maximum Flow and the Maximum Weight Matching problems, notice that the whole scheme transforms the problem instance into an adequate form and then computes a maximum matching for the last graph in RNC. We can compute and approximate matching using the NCAS for matching. Using adequate error parameters for both algorithms we can control the total error, thus we get

Theorem 5.2.2 *The* Maximum Flow *problem and the* Maximum Weight Matching *problem are in* NCAS.

Given a collection C of subsets of a finite set S, and an integer k such that $0 < k \leq |C|$, the Set Cover problem asks if there exists a $C' \subseteq C$, with $|C'| \leq k$, such that every element of S belongs to at least one member of C.

The Set Cover problem can be formulated as an integer program,

$$\begin{cases} \min \sum_{j=1}^{n} x_j, \\ Ax \leq 1_m, \\ x_j \in \{0, 1\} \text{ for } j = 1, \dots, n. \end{cases}$$

In the previous formulation, we have a variable for each set and the matrix A gives the membership relation between elements and sets. Recall that the linear programming relaxation of the above formulation allows us to obtain an approximation within a $\log n$ factor [PS82], furthermore it corresponds to a positive linear program, again further improvements are needed in order to get the approximate set cover, using ideas from [Rag88] thus we get

Theorem 5.2.3 (Luby, Nisan) *The* Set Cover *problem can be approximated in NC, within a* $(1 + \epsilon) \log n$ *factor.*

5.3 The Vertex Cover Problem

The primal–dual technique can also be paralellized when dealing with a problem that has specific approximate complementary slackness conditions. In particular we consider the algorithm by Khuller, Vishkin and Young [KVY93] for approximating the Minimum Weight Vertex Cover problem on hypergraphs and its dual one, the Maximum Weight Edge Packing problem.

Let $G = (V, E)$, $E \subseteq 2^V$ be a given undirected hypergraph with vertex weights $w : V \to \mathbb{R}^+$. Let $E(v)$ denote the set of edges adjacent to vertex v. Let G have m edges. Let r be the maximum size of any edge, and let M be the sum of the edge sizes.

As a consequence of the linear programming duality, we have that the weight of any cover is at least the weight of any packing.

Lemma 5.3.1 (Duality) *Given a hypergraph G, let C be an arbitrary vertex cover and p an arbitrary edge packing. Then $p(E) \leq w(C)$.*

The next result states that when every vertex in C has its dual constraint nearly met by p, then $w(C)$ is at most a factor times $p(E)$.

Lemma 5.3.2 (Approximate Complementary Slackness) *Given a hypergraph G, let C be a vertex cover and p be a packing such that $p(E(v)) \geq (1 - \epsilon)w(v)$ for every $v \in C$. Then $(1 - \epsilon)w(C) \leq r\, p(E)$. By duality, the*

weights of C and p are within a factor of $r/(1 - \epsilon)$ from their respective optima.

Proof Since $(1 - \epsilon)w(v) \leq p(E(v))$ for all $v \in C$,

$$(1 - \epsilon)w(C) = (1 - \epsilon)\sum_{v \in C} w(v) \leq \sum_{v \in C} p(E(V)) = \sum_{e \in E} |e \cap C| p(e) \leq r\,p(E).$$

$\square$

The above lemma can be tightened when the weights are integers:

Lemma 5.3.3 *In the previous lemma, if the weights are integers and $\epsilon < 1/w(V)$, then the weight of C is at most r times the minimum.*

Given a packing p, define $C_p = \{v \in V \mid p(E(v)) \geq (1 - \epsilon)w(v)\}$. When C_p is a vertex cover packing p is said to be ϵ-maximal. Thus the problem is reduced to finding an ϵ-maximal packing. The algorithm mantains a packing p and the partial cover C_p. The algorithm increases the individual $p(e)$'s until p is an ϵ-maximal packing.

COVER $(G = (V, E), w, \epsilon)$
1   **for all** $v \in V$ **pardo**
       $w_p(v) := w(v); E_p(v) := E(v); d_p(v) := |E(v)|;$
2   **while** edges remain **do**
3   **for all** remaining edges e **pardo**
           $\delta(e) := min_{v \in e} w_p(v)/d_p(v);$
4   **for all** remaining vertices v **pardo**
5           $w_p(v) := w_p(v) - \sum_{e \in E_p(v)} \delta(e);$
6   **if** $w_p(v) \leq \epsilon w(v)$**then**
7   delete v and incident edges, updating E_p and d_p;
8   **return** the set of deleted vertices

Algorithm 16: NC-approximetion for Vertex Cover

Let us show that Algorithm 16 takes time $O(r \ln^2 m \ln(1/\epsilon))$. We use a potential function argument. Given a packing p, define

$$\Phi_p = \sum_{v \in V} d_p(v) \ln \frac{w_p(v)}{\epsilon\,w(v)}.$$

The next lemma shows that during an iteration of the **while** loop Φ_p decreases by at least the number of edges remaining at the end of the loop.

Lemma 5.3.4 *Let p and p', respectively, be the packing before and after an iteration of the **while** loop. Then $|\Phi_p - \Phi_{p'}| \geq |E'_p|$.*

Proof During the iteration, we say that a vertex v limits an incident edge $e \in E_p$ if v determines the minimum in the computation of $\min_{v \in e}\{w_p(v)/d_p(v)\}$. For each vertex v, let v limit $L(v)$ edges, so that $w_{p'}(v) \leq w_p(v)(1 - L(v)/d_p(v))$. Let V' denote the set of vertices that remain after the iteration. Then

$$\Phi_p - \Phi_{p'} = \sum_{v \in V}\left(d_p(v)\ln\frac{w_p(v)}{\epsilon\,w(v)} - d_{p'}(v)\ln\frac{w_{p'}(v)}{\epsilon\,w(v)}\right)$$

$$\geq \sum_{v \in V'}d_p(v)\ln\frac{w_p(v)}{\epsilon\,w(v)}$$

$$\geq \sum_{v \in V'}-d_p(v)\ln(1 - L(v)/d_p(v))$$

$$\geq \sum_{v \in V'}L(v)$$

$$\geq |E_{p'}|.$$

The second-to-last step follows because $-\ln(1-x) \geq x$. The last step follows because each of the edges that remains is limited by some vertex in V'. □

We can bound the number of iterations,

Lemma 5.3.5 *There are at most $O((1 + \ln m)(1 + r\ln(1/\epsilon)))$ iterations.*

Proof Let p and p', respectively, be the packing before and after any iteration. Let $a = r\ln(1/\epsilon)$. Clearly $\Phi_{p'} \leq |E_{p'}|a$. By the previous lemma $\Phi_{p'} \leq \Phi_p - |E_{p'}|$. Thus $\Phi_{p'} \leq \Phi_p(1 - 1/(a+1))$. Before the first iteration, $\Phi_p \leq ma$. Then inductively, before the ith iteration,

$$\Phi_p \leq ma(1 - 1/(a+1))^{i-1} \leq ma\,\exp(-(i-1)/(a+1)).$$

The last inequality follows from $e^x \geq 1 + x$ for all x. Fixing $i = 1 + \lceil(a+1)\ln m\rceil$, we have $\exp(-(i-1)/(a+1)) \leq \exp(-\ln m) = 1/m$, so before the ith iteration, $\Phi_p \leq a$. During each subsequent iteration, at least one edge remains, so Φ_p decreases by at least 1. So $\Phi_p \leq 0$ before an $(i+a)$th iteration can occur. □

Recall that an iteration with q edges requires $O(r\,q)$ operations. Thus the total number of operations is bounded by an amount proportional to r times the sum, over all iterations, of the number of edges at the beginning of that iteration. By Lemma 5.3.4, in a given iteration, Φ_p decreases by at least the number of edges remaining at the end of the iteration. Thus the sum over all iterations of the number of edges during the iteration is at most $m + \Phi_p$ for the initial p. This is $m + M \ln(1/\epsilon)$ operations. Using Brent's scheduling principle the operations can be efficiently scheduled in $M/\ln^2 m$ processors. This stablishes the main theorem,

Theorem 5.3.6 *Algorithm 16 uses $O(r \ln^2 m \ln(1/\epsilon))$ parallel steps and $M/\ln^2 m$ processors. Furthermore, the algorithm returns a vertex cover of weight at most $r/(1 - \epsilon)$ times the minimum weight.*

Therefore Algorithm COVER is an NC approximation for the Weighted Vertex Cover problem. Notice that when G has $r = 2$, the algorithm returns a vertex cover of weight within a factor of $2/(1 - \epsilon)$ of the optimum.

6

Graph Decomposition

For some graph problems, the fact of restricting the input to planar graphs simplifies the computational complexity of the problem. However, there are some NP-complete problems that remain NP-complete even when restricted to planar graphs, for instance the Maximum Independent Set problem (see [GJ79]). We have already mentioned in the introduction that to find a constant approximation to the problem of the Maximum Independent Set for a general graph with n vertices is as difficult as to find an approximation to the problem of finding a Maximum Clique, which means that unless P=NP, the Maximum Independent Set problem cannot be approximated within $n^{1-\epsilon}$ [Has96].

Baker ([Bak83], [Bak94]) took advantage of a particular way of decomposing planar graphs to produce approximation schemes for some problems that for general graphs were difficult to approximate, among them the Maximum Independent Set problem. The idea of her method is, given a problem on a planar graph, to choose a fixed k and decompose the graph into k-outerplanar graphs (see below for the basic definitions on planar graphs), then using dynamic programming techniques obtain the exact solution to the problem for each of the k-outerplanar graphs. For each k, an adequate decomposition of the graph into k-outerplanar subgraphs gives a $k/(k+1)$ approximation to the optimal. Moreover it could be implemented in polynomial time. Taking $k = O(c \log n)$ where c is some constant, a Polynomial Time Approximation Scheme is obtained. Using the above technique, Baker was able to produce Polynomial Time Approximation Schemes for a set of problems on planar graphs. The most significant of them is the Maximum Independent Set problem. Other problems that can be seen in PTAS using the above technique are the Minimum Vertex Cover, the Minimum Dominating Set, the Minimum Edge Dominating Set, and others (see the appendix in [Bak94]). Baker's technique was not the first one to obtain an approximation scheme for the Maximum Independent Set problem on planar graphs. Lipton and Tarjan [LT80] used their *planar separator theorem* [LT79], to get a time $O(n \log n)$ approximation scheme for the problem. Unfortunately to obtain a good approximation ratio with $0 < \epsilon < 1$, a value of n larger than double exponential in $1/\epsilon$ is needed. Therefore the algorithm of Baker obtained better bounds, moreover the method of Baker is sufficiently general to obtain Polynomial Time Approximation Schemes for a whole set of NP-hard planar graph problems.

Some problems on planar graphs were previously known to be in APX. For instance, Chiba, Nishizeki and Saito, using a previously developed 5-coloring algorithm for planar graphs, presented an $O(n \log n)$ algorithm for the Maximum Independent Set problem on planar graphs with a 1/5 ratio of approximation [CNS82]. Based on their algorithm, Chrobak and Naor gave a NC algorithm to obtain a $\frac{1}{2}$-approximation to the aximum Independent Set problem on planar graphs, in parallel time $O(\log^2 n)$ and using an amount of work $O(n \log^2 n)$ [CN89]. Thus they put the Maximum Independent Set problem for planar graphs in the class NCX.

Díaz, Serna and Torán gave a parallel method, to put most of the planar graph problems known to be in PTAS in the class NCAS ([DST93], [DST96]). Although their method follows the same general scheme as [Bak94], the techniques they use are different, in particular they introduce original methods to obtain in parallel a representation of the k-outerplanar graphs as binary trees. The dynamic programming part in Baker's proof is translated into a shunt operation in the binary tree representing the graphs.

6.1 Planar Graphs

Let us give some basic terminology for planar graphs. Given an undirected graph $G = (V, E)$ an **subgraph induced** by a set of vertices is formed by these vertices and every edge in E between them. The **connected components** of a disconnected graph are its maximal connected subgraphs. An **articulation point** (or **cutpoint**) in a connected graph is a vertex v such that the graph obtained by removing v (and its incident edges) has at least two connected components. A **bridge** in a connected graph is an edge $e = (u, v)$ such that the graph obtained by removing e has at least two connected components. A **biconnected** graph is a connected graph containing no articulation point. Through the remaining part of the chapter, we shall be talking about undirected connected graphs.

A **planar embedding** of an undirected graph $G = (V, E)$ is a function $\mathcal{G}$ that maps the vertices of G to distinct points in $\mathbb{R}^2$ and each edge $(u, v) \in E$

to a Jordan curve in $\mathbb{R}^2$ from $\mathcal{G}(u)$ to $\mathcal{G}(v)$ such that for all $e = (u, v) \in E$, $\mathcal{G}(e) \cap (\mathcal{G}(V) \cup \mathcal{G}(E - e)) = \{\mathcal{G}(u), \mathcal{G}(v)\}$. A graph G is **planar** if there exists a planar embedding of G. Let $\mathcal{G}$ be a planar embedding of G. The **faces** of $\mathcal{G}$ are the connected regions of $\mathbb{R}^2 - \mathcal{G}(V \cup E)$. Let $\mathcal{F}$ denote the set of faces in $\mathcal{G}$, and let f_∞ denote the **exterior face** of $\mathcal{G}$. Two faces of $\mathcal{G}$ are said to be **adjacent** if they share at least one edge of E. The **exterior boundary** $\mathcal{B}$ of $\mathcal{G}$ is the set of edges separating f_∞ from the other faces of $\mathcal{G}$.

There are several sequential algorithms to find a plane embedding of a planar graph. A particularly efficient approach uses a specific data structure to represent planar graphs, the PQ-tree due to Booth and Lueker [BL76] (see also chapter 3 of the book by Nishizeki and Chiba [NC88]). In the parallel setting, JáJá and Simon gave a parallel algorithm to test planarity [JS82]. They reduced the problem of planarity testing to the problem of solving linear systems. Although the paper was the first to show that the problem of deciding planarity of a graph is in NC, their method had two drawbacks. First the algorithm was unfeasible due to the large amount of processors needed, second their algorithm finds a planar embedding for tri-connected graphs but not for arbitrary graphs. Later on, Klein and Reif gave a parallel algorithm to test if a graph is planar, and in the affirmative case find a planar embedding [KR86]. For a graph on n vertices, their algorithm runs in $O(\log^2 n)$ steps and with work $O(n \log^2 n)$, and makes use of the PQ-trees data structure, complemented with new operations defined on the data structure, which are convenient to handle the PQ-trees in parallel. Finally, Ramachandran and Reif gave an optimal parallel algorithm to find a planar embedding of a planar graph [RR89]. They use the ear decomposition technique (see for instance section 5.4 of the book by JáJá [JaJ92]). The algorithms described in this chapter assume that the plane graph can be found using any of the feasible PRAM algorithms referenced above.

Through the remainder of the chapter, the term **embedded graph** will denote a planar graph G together with a particular planar embedding of G. The usual way to give an embedding of a graph is by the cyclic (counterclockwise) order of edges around each vertex, together with the exterior face. Notice that in a planar graph $|E| = O(n)$. In the following we will assume that a planar graph G is given as a list of vertices and for each vertex a linked list of its neighbors, in the order specified by the embedding.

Given an embedded graph G, its **quasidual graph** $G^* = (V^*, E^*)$ is the graph whose vertex set is the set $\{\mathcal{F} - f_\infty\} \cup \mathcal{B}$ and for any two faces $f_1, f_2 \in \mathcal{F} - f_\infty$, $(f_1, f_2) \in E^*$ iff both faces are adjacent, and for any face $f \in \mathcal{F} - f_\infty$ and any $e \in \mathcal{B}$, $(f, e) \in E^*$ if and only if e separates f and f_∞. Given an embedded graph G, the **face incidence graph** $G^+ = (V^+, E^+)$

is the graph whose vertex set is the set $\mathcal{F}$ of faces of G, and for any two faces $f_1 \neq f_2$, $(f_1, f_2) \in E^+$ exactly if f_1 and f_2 have at least one vertex in common. For any face $f \in V^+$ let $d(f)$ be the minimum distance from f to the node representing the exterior face in G^+.

Theorem 6.1.1 *Given an embedded graph G, its face incidence graph can be computed in parallel time $O(\log n)$ using $O(n^2)$ processors.*

Proof We use Algorithm 17 to construct G^+.

FACE-INCIDENCE(G)
1 For each edge in G consider two directed edges (one in each direction).
2 Construct the matrix $M(i, j)$ defined by $M(i, j) = (j, k)$ if k is the vertex next to i in the adjacency list of j.
3 The graph associated to M is a disjoint union of cycles, each cycle corresponding to a face of G. Using pointer jumping assign a name to each face (for example the largest number of a processor assigned to an edge of the face).
4 To get G^+, we only need to test for each pair of faces whether they share a vertex.

Algorithm 17: Construction of G^+

Notice that in step 2 the matrix M can be obtained in constant time using $O(n)$ processors, because a planar graph has $O(n)$ edges. Furthermore step 4 can be done in $O(\log n)$ time with $O(n^2)$ processors. The remaining steps can be trivially implemented in the given bounds. □

A vertex is a **level 1** vertex if it is on the exterior face. Let G^i be the graph obtained by deleting all vertices in levels 1 to i, then the vertices on the exterior face of G^i are the **level $i + 1$** vertices.

An embedded graph is k-**outerplanar** if it has no vertices of level greater than k (see Figure 6.1). Every embedded graph is k-outerplanar for some k. The terms outerplanar and 1-outerplanar are equivalent.

We show now how to compute in parallel the levels of a connected embedded graph G. Without lost of generality we assume that the planar graph is

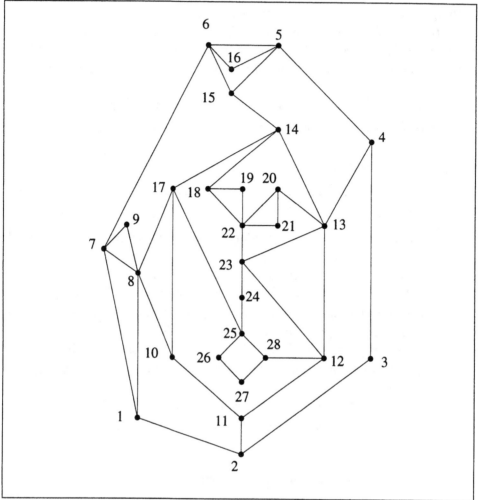

Fig. 6.1: A 3-outerplanar graph G

biconnected. Observe that since the plane embedding of G is obtained from plane embeddings of its biconnected components, the level of each node is independent for each component.

Lemma 6.1.2 *Given an embedded graph G and its face incidence graph G^{+}, for any face f, $d(f) = k$ if and only if f contains at least one level k vertex and the remaining vertices in f are level k or $k + 1$ vertices.*

Proof First note that as G is biconnected every vertex lies in at least two faces. Furthermore, a face cannot have vertices in more than two levels, according to the definition of level.

For a given face f, let $l(f)$ be the lowest level of a vertex in f. The definition of face adjacency insures that when (f_1, f_2) is an edge in the face incidence graph G^+ then $| l(f_1) - l(f_2) | \leq 1$. Thus carrying on a trivial induction proof, we get $l(f) = d(f)$. $\qquad\square$

As a corollary we get the following way to compute the level of a vertex.

Corollary 6.1.3 *Given an embedded graph G, for each vertex v of G, the level of vertex v in G is given by $l(v) = 1 + \min_{v \in f} d(f)$.*

Thus we reduce the problem of assigning a level number to each vertex of a planar graph to the problem of computing distances in the face incidence graph, thus we get the following bounds.

Theorem 6.1.4 *Given an embedded graph G, the level of each vertex can be computed in parallel time $O(\log^2 n)$ using $O(n^3)$ processors.*

Proof We first construct the face incidence graph G^+, according to the algorithm in the proof of the previous theorem. Then, using transitive closure we compute the distances to the exterior face in $O(\log^2 n)$ time using $O(n^3)$ processors (see for example [JaJ92]). Finally the minimum distance of the faces containing a given vertex can be computed in $O(\log n)$ time and with $O(n)$ processors. $\qquad\square$

From now on, we assume that all the faces in the embedded graph are identified with its numbering. In order to simplify the notation we will use the term **level i subgraph** to denote a connected component of the subgraph induced by the level i vertices (see Figure 6.2).

It follows from the definition of levels that every level subgraph is outerplanar. Furthermore, every level $i + 1$ subgraph is in a face of a level i subgraph, but there can be faces in a level i subgraph that do not contain any level $i + 1$ subgraph, for instance face 8-10-17 in Figure 6.2. A face in a level i subgraph can have inside more than one level $i + 1$ subgraph. If this is the case, we add dummy edges to G to split the face in such a way that each new face contains exactly one level i subgraph, taking care to preserve the planarity. For instance, in Figure 6.2 the unique level 1 face has inside two level 2 subgraphs, one formed by vertex 16 and the other formed by the remaining vertices at level 2. Therefore from now on, we assume that inside of each face at level i there is at most one level $i + 1$ subgraph.

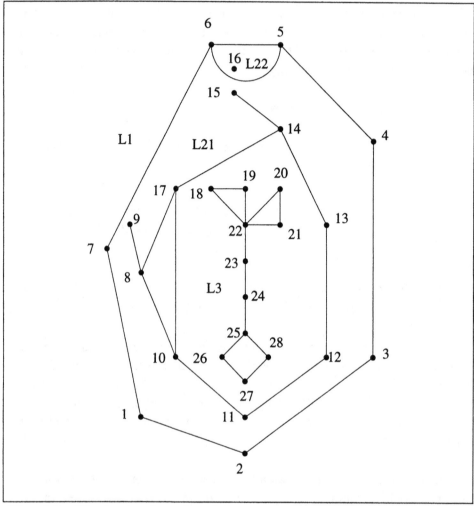

Fig. 6.2: The level subgraphs of the graph G. Dummy edges have been added in order to have at most one level subgraph inside a face.

6.2 The Maximum Independent Set for Outerplanar Graphs

Let us assume that we are given a biconnected outerplanar graph G' (we use G' to differentiate from planar non-biconnected graphs G). The **face–face tree** representation of G' is a rooted ordered tree that has as leaves the edges in the exterior boundary of G', and constructed in such a way that each internal node x in the tree corresponds to an interior face f_x of G'. In fact for every interior node x of the tree, we can associate two vertices of G', $b_1(x)$ and $b_2(x)$ such that if y denotes the parent of x in the tree, then $(b_1(x), b_2(x))$ is the interior edge of G' separating f_x from f_y. Moreover

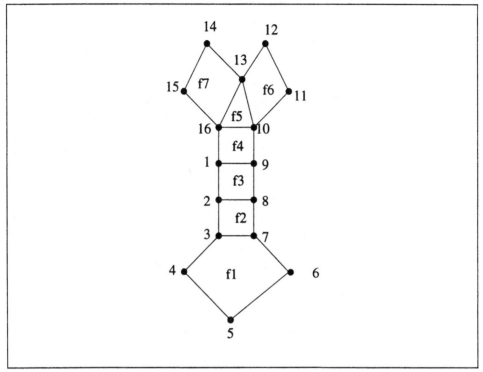

Fig. 6.3: A biconnected outerplanar graph G'

we also identify x with the portion of the graph G'_x induced by all nodes encountered in a counterclockwise tour on the exterior face of G', starting at $b_1(x)$ and ending at $b_2(x)$. In the case of the root r, we have $b_1(r) = b_2(r)$, so that $G'_r = G'$.

It should be clear that for any node x, a preorder traversal of the subtree rooted at x gives a counterclockwise traversal of the exterior face G'_x, starting at $b_1(x)$ and ending at $b_2(x)$. Figure 6.4 presents the face–face tree corresponding to the biconnected graph in Figure 6.3.

Lemma 6.2.1 *Given a biconnected outerplanar graph G' a face–face tree representation can be obtained in $O(\log n)$ parallel time using $O(n^2)$ processors.*

Proof Given G', in parallel construct its quasidual graph G'^* in $O(\log n)$ time and using $O(n)$ processors. Notice that G'^* is a unrooted tree and the leaves are vertices labeled as boundary edges of G'. Choose an interior vertex of G'^* as root r and choose any vertex of the face in G' represented by r as $b(r)$. Obtain the rooted face–face tree representation using pointer

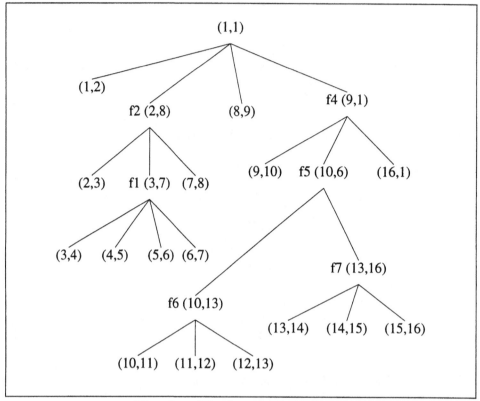

Fig. 6.4: The face–face tree of G'

jumping. We associate to each node different from r the edge (in G') shared with the face represented by its parent, with the corresponding orientation. The parallel complexity of the tree construction is $O(\log n)$ steps with $O(n^2)$ processors.   □

In order to construct the face–face tree of an outerplanar (not necessarily biconnected) graph G, we first transform G into a biconnected outerplanar graph G'. After, use the tree representation of G' as tree representation for G. The construction of G' from G is done by Algorithm 18.

Figure 6.5 shows two examples of the transformation described, and Figure 6.6 shows other examples without the drawing of the intermediate steps. Figure 6.3 presents the transformation corresponding to the level 3 subgraph in Figure 6.2. The extension from G to G' increases the number of vertices (and hence of edges) only by a constant factor. The G' constructed has no cutpoints, so is a biconnected graph. Also all new edges lie on the new exterior face, preserving outerplanarity. To keep information about G in G' we will classify the edges of the G' constructed into two types; **virtual**

CONSTRUCT(G)

1 For each cutpoint p of G whose removal gives $k \geq 2$ components, we add k vertices connected as a cycle. (In the case $k = 2$, added vertices just form an edge.) Every interior face having p as cutpoint will be glued to one different edge on the cycle, and every single edge in G having p as endpoint will be transformed into a new edge. (Notice that the point itself expands into a new interior face of G' delimited by the cycle.) The planar embedding gives a cyclic order of the edges from p, giving also a cyclic ordering of the components. The new vertices will follow this order, each vertex will be attached to two consecutive components, and connected to the last vertex in the first component and to all vertices previous to the last (if any) in the next component.

2 After this step every edge from p has a copy as an edge from some of the new nodes in the neighborhood of p. Moreover, each bridge has been converted into four nodes (two from each endpoint), we connect the endpoints by two parallel edges.

3 Finally we remove all vertices that were cutpoints in G with the corresponding edges.

Algorithm 18: Constructing G'

edges that are the edges joining two vertices in G' corresponding to the same vertex in G, and **real** edges that are all the remaining edges in G'.

Lemma 6.2.2 *Given an outerplanar graph G, the associated biconnected graph G' can be obtained in parallel time $O(\log^2 n)$ and using $O(n^2)$ processors.*

Proof Obtain the list of cutpoints and bridges of G together with the number of connected components for each cutpoint. This can be done in parallel time $O(\log^2 n)$ using $O(n^2)$ processors [HCS79]. Once we have the list, the new graph G' can be obtained in constant parallel time using $O(n)$ processors. $\qquad\square$

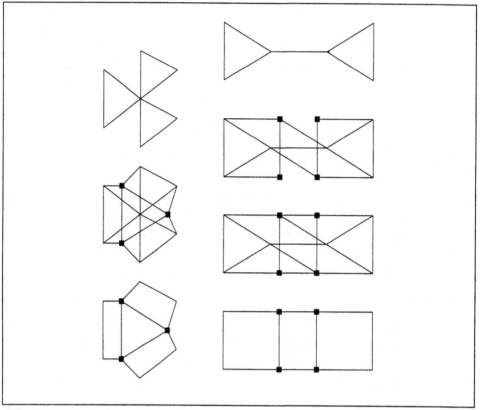

Fig. 6.5: Transformation of a cutpoint with three components and a bridge

It is easy to verify that the face–face tree for G' also satisfies all the required conditions for the outerplanar graph G.

Lemma 6.2.3 *Given an outerplanar graph G and the associated biconnected graph G', a tree representation of G can be obtained in parallel time $O(\log n)$ and using $O(n^2)$ processors.*

As a last step, we have to convert the face–face tree representation into a binary tree (this step is necessary to apply the tree-contraction technique). The conversion can be done in $O(\log n)$ parallel steps using a linear number of processors [ADKP89]. As usual, during the transformation from non-binary to binary, we need to add some extra dummy nodes (without meaning with respect to the topology of G'). All the remaining nodes in the binary tree representation are also nodes in the non-binary tree representation and they are associated with an edge (b_1, b_2) of G'. The non-dummy nodes of the binary tree representation can be further classified into two types. A

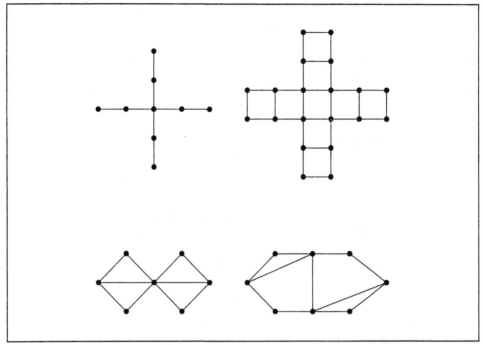

Fig. 6.6: The associated graph for some outerplanar graphs

node x is said to be **virtual** if $(b_1(x), b_2(x))$ is a virtual edge of G' that also is a vertex in G, otherwise x is said to be **real**. Observe that the leaves of the tree can be either real or virtual, and the internal nodes can be any of the three types. Moreover, the root r of the tree will be classified as virtual node (see Figure 6.7, where the black spots represent dummy nodes, the black squares represent virtual nodes and the remainder are real nodes).

Given a binary face–face tree, we compute the Maximum Independent Set of the corresponding outerplanar graph. Recall that by construction, to each node x in the tree we have associated two vertices $b_1(x), b_2(x)$, and a subgraph G_x of the graph G. Moreover we associate to each node x in the tree a table t_x with four entries: $t_x(0,0), t_x(0,1), t_x(1,0)$ and $t_x(1,1)$. Each entry contains the maximum size of an independent set in G_x depending on which of the associated vertices are or are not required to be in the independent set. Thus $t_x(0,0)$ contains the maximum size of an independent set not containing both $b_1(x)$ and $b_2(x)$; $t_x(0,1)$ contains the maximum size of an independent set not containing $b_1(x)$ but containing $b_2(x)$; $t_x(1,0)$ contains the maximum size of an independent set not containing $b_2(x)$ but containing $b_1(x)$; finally $t_x(1,1)$ contains the maximum size of an independent set containing both $b_1(x)$ and $b_2(x)$.

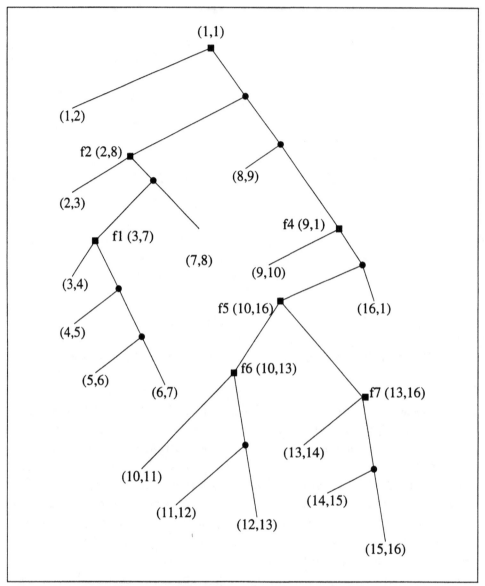

Fig. 6.7: The binary face–face tree of L_3

For a real leaf x the corresponding table is easy to compute, note that G_x is just an edge, thus we let $t_x(0,0) = 0$, $t_x(0,1) = t_x(1,0) = 1$ and $t_x(1,1)$ is undefined (there is no independent set containing both endpoints). If the leaf is virtual, the associated table is defined as $t_x(0,0) = 0$, $t_x(1,1) = 1$, with $t_x(0,1)$ and $t_x(1,0)$ undefined.

To compute the Maximum Independent Set for the whole outerplanar graph, we traverse the tree in a bottom-up way, computing at each interior node of the tree an operation **merge** of tables. As we have three types of internal nodes we need three types of merging. The basic merge of two tables t_x and t_y is defined using a dynamic programming operation: for any $a, b \in \{0, 1\}$

$$t_{xy}(a, b) = \max_{c \in \{0,1\}} \{t_x(a, c) + t_y(c, b) - c\}.$$

Suppose that z is an internal node with left child x and right child y, the table for z will be $t_z = t_{xy}$ when z is a dummy node, $t_z = t_{xy}$ except for the entry $(1, 1)$ which will be undefined when z is real, and when z is virtual $t_z(0, 0) = t_{xy}(0, 0)$, $t_z(1, 1) = t_{xy}(1, 1) - 1$, while the other entries remain undefined.

An induction proof shows that the table obtained for each internal node corresponds to the maximum size of an independent set for the associated subgraph. Once we have a table for the root, the two entries in this table (recall that the root is a virtual node) give us the maximum size of an independent set for G including the associated vertex or not, thus taking the maximum of both entries we get the size of a Maximum Independent Set for the graph G. In Figure 6.8 is given the computation for the tree given in Figure 6.7, a table is represented by a vector with four components corresponding to the entrances 00, 01, 10, and 11 respectively.

We define now the **shunt** operation in the tree-contraction technique. Suppose that x is the leaf which is ready to perform the shunt, that z is its parent and that y is the other child of z. We will contract the three nodes into a single one. Clearly for any internal node, the piece of the graph represented after the contraction will have three contact vertices, so that we have to keep a three-entry table in the internal contracted nodes. To define the new operation we proceed by cases. In order to simplify the definitions we assume that x is the left child of z, and that when we have a three-entry table, the first and the second entries correspond to the vertices shared with the left child, the second and the third with the right child, and the first and the last with the parent. Furthermore the phrase "*incorporate the type of node x*" into a table has the following meaning: If x is real, the value corresponding to $(1,1)$ will be undefined; if x is virtual, all values corresponding to $(1,0)$ and $(0,1)$ will be undefined, and we subtract 1 from all values corresponding to $(1,1)$; in case $(0,0)$ the table is not modified. We distinguish two cases:

Case 1. z is a node that has not been processed by the shunt operation, thus z contains only information about the type of an edge.

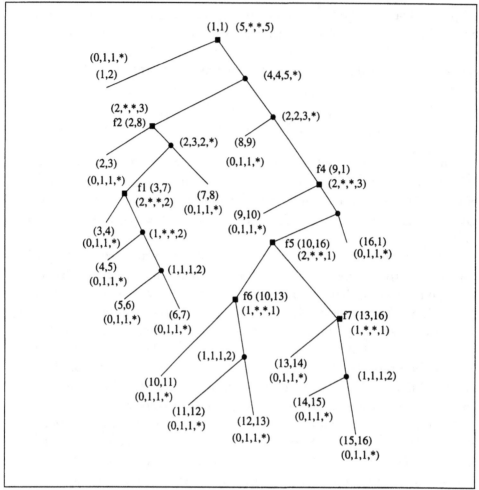

Fig. 6.8: Computing the Maximum Independent Set size

Case 1.1. y is a leaf, using the corresponding merging we get a two-entry table for z, note that now z becomes a leaf.

Case 1.2. y is not a leaf and has not been processed by the shunt operation. In this case we construct a three-entry table as follows:

$$t_{xyz}(a, b, c) = t_x(a, b) + c$$

for $a, b, c \in \{0, 1\}$. After that, we incorporate the type of nodes y and z.

Case 1.3. y is not a leaf but a node obtained after a shunt. In this case y has a three-entry table, and we construct a three-entry table as follows:

$$t_{xyz}(a, b, c) = \max_{d \in \{0,1\}} \{t_x(a, d) + t_y(d, b, c) - d\}$$

for $a, b, c \in \{0, 1\}$. After that, we incorporate the type of node z.

Case 2. z is a node obtained after a shunt, now z has a table with three entries.

Case 2.1. Node y is a leaf, and thus have a two-entry table. The resulting graph has only two associated vertices. Again the new node will be a leaf. We construct a table as follows:

$$t_{xyz}(a, b) = \max_{c \in \{0,1\}} \{t_x(a, c) + t_z(a, c, b) + t_y(c, b) - c\} - a - b$$

for $a, b \in \{0, 1\}$.

Case 2.2. Node y is neither a leaf nor a node processed by the shunt operation. In this case we construct the new table as follows:

$$t_{xyz}(a, b, c) = t_x(a, b) + t_z(a, b, c) - a - b$$

for $a, b, c \in \{0, 1\}$. After that, we incorporate the type of node y.

Case 2.3. Node y is not a leaf but a node obtained as result of the shunt. In this case y has a three-entry table computed as follows:

$$t_{xyz}(a, b, c) = \max_{d \in \{0,1\}} \{t_x(a, d) + t_z(a, d, b) + t_y(d, c, b) - 2d\} - a - b$$

for $a, b, c \in \{0, 1\}$.

It is easy to show that in each case the values contained in each entry correspond to the maximum size of independent sets for the corresponding subgraph, taking into account the associated vertices that are required to be in the independent set.

Each one of the operations can be computed in constant parallel time using a constant number of processors, thus using the tree-contraction technique we can compute the final Maximum Independent Set in $O(\log n)$ parallel time using $O(n)$ processors. However, the resources needed are dominated by the step in which we construct the associated biconnected outerplanar graph. Therefore we have

Theorem 6.2.4 *There is a parallel algorithm to solve the* Maximum Independent Set *problem for outerplanar graphs running in* $O(\log^2 n)$ *time and using* $O(n^2)$ *processors.*

6.3 The Maximum Independent Set for k-Outerplanar Graphs

We obtained in parallel a tree representation of a connected k-outerplanar graph. In this representation we will keep information on each of the level subgraphs (a face–face tree as presented before) but now the graph associated with an internal node at level i in the face–face tree will be a subgraph of the graph induced by all nodes in levels 1 to i.

Given a k-outerplanar graph G, we convert it into an associated graph G'' with the property that each level subgraph is biconnected. We proceed in parallel for each level subgraph, using the procedure described in the previous section. (Recall that for a given value of i, we may have more than one level i subgraph, each of those is treated separately.) When we copy part of the edges from a given cutpoint, we also include the edges joining this cutpoint to the previous level. Notice that an edge joining two cutpoints of two different levels has been converted into two edges, each one connecting a cutpoint with a new edge, we connect both new vertices (see Figure 6.9). Finally we remove all vertices that were cutpoints in a level subgraph. The graph associated to Figure 6.1 is given in Figure 6.10.

To construct the face–face tree for the whole graph, we begin by constructing the face–face tree for each level subgraph. As each level i subgraph is inside a face of a level $i - 1$ subgraph, we know from where to hang the tree; however, it is necessary to choose appropriately the roots of the different face–face trees, so when the tree for the whole level k subgraph is constructed, it will have the desired properties. Let us start with a definition. A level vertex v in a subgraph at level i is said to be **consistent** with a vertex u in a subgraph at level $i-1$ (respectively a level $i-1$ edge e) if the two vertices (the vertex and the middle point of the edge) can be joined by a line preserving planarity, taking into account the edges between different levels. A **consistent set of roots** is a selection of pairs (face,vertex), where the vertex has to be in the face, one for each level subgraph, such that after constructing the corresponding face–face trees, each root of a level i (for $i > 1$) tree is consistent with the edge (vertex) associated to the enclosing face. For the graph in Figure 6.10 nodes 6, 14 and 23 form a consistent set of roots.

Lemma 6.3.1 *A consistent set of roots can be constructed in $O(\log n)$ parallel time using $O(n^2)$ processors.*

Proof To choose in parallel the roots of the level trees, we construct an auxiliary graph. This graph has the following set of nodes: all pairs (f, v) with f a face in a level subgraph of G'' and such that v belongs to f, together

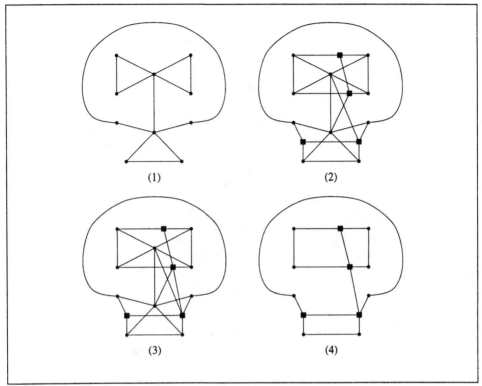

Fig. 6.9: The transformation of an edge joining two cutpoints in different levels

with all pairs (f, e) where f is a face in a level subgraph and e is an interior edge of the subgraph such that e belongs to f. The set of edges are the pairs:

> $((f, v), (f', e))$ where f and f' are different faces in the same level i subgraph with e being the closing edge of f' in a counterclokwise traversal starting at v. Notice that when f and f' are neighbors and v is common to both faces, then e will be the boundary between f and f'.
>
> $((f, e), (f', v))$ where f' and v are a level $i + 1$ face and vertex, f is the corresponding enclosing face in the level i subgraph, e is an edge in f, and v and e are consistent.
>
> $((f, v), (f', v'))$ where f' and v' are a level $i + 1$ face and vertex, f is the corresponding enclosing face in the level i subgraph, v is a vertex in f, and v and v' are consistent.

The whole auxiliary graph looks like a $2k - 1$ layered graph. The first two layers correspond to the bipartite graph between (f, v) and (f', e) at

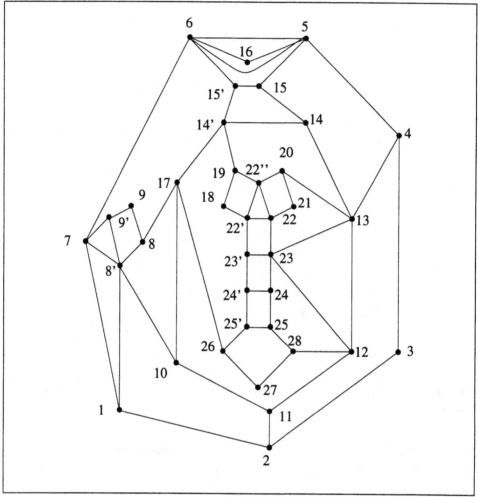

Fig. 6.10: The associated graph G''

level one of G''. Successive layers alternate between bipartite graphs representing correct possible connections between levels and correct face–face subtree for a subgraph of the same level, and bipartite graphs representing correct connections between face–face subtrees for different levels in G''. Moreover, by construction the auxiliary graph will have $O(n)$ vertices. This graph can be constructed in $O(\log n)$ parallel time using $O(n^2)$ processors.

From the previous construction, to select in parallel a consistent set of roots for the level trees, for each node (f, e), corresponding to a level i face, we choose one of the existing edges (if any) joining this node with a level $i + 1$ vertex. By choosing only a level 1 (vertex, face) pair, we get a

v	23	24	25	26	27	28	25'	24'	23'	22"	21
d(v)	14	14	17	17	17	12	12	12	13	13	13

v	20	22'	19	18	22	23	16	16	14	17	18'
d(v)	13	13	13	14	14	14	5	6	6	6	6

v	9'	9	8	10	11	12	13	14'	15'	15	14
d(v)	6	7	1	1	2	2	4	4	5	6	6

Fig. 6.11: d-values for the nodes in G''

tree, the set of all pairs (vertex, face) in this tree form a consistent set of roots. $\qquad\square$

Once we have a consistent set of roots, we construct the face–face trees. We want to relate vertices in a given face–face tree of a subgraph level to vertices in the enclosing face in such a way that the resulting tree has the desired properties.

For a given face–face level i (for $i > 1$) tree T, let $a_1, \ldots, a_s$ be the exterior cycle of edges at level i going from the first endpoint to the last (that is the exterior boundary of the corresponding subgraph), and $d_1, \ldots, d_q$ be the path (cycle) of level $i - 1$ edges in the enclosing face. To each vertex v we associate a vertex $d(v)$ in the enclosing face defined as follows. Let v_0 be the first vertex of a_1, v_i be the common vertex of a_{i-1} and a_i, and v_{s+1} be the last vertex of a_s. (Notice that v_0 and v_{s+1} are in fact the same vertex but are considered different as first and last vertices on the tour.) Then $d(v_0)$ is the first vertex of d_1 and $d(v_{s+1})$ is the last vertex of d_q. For other i we consider two cases: v_i has no edges to vertices in the enclosing face, if this is the case $d(v_i) = d(v_{i-1})$, otherwise $d(v_i) = w$ where w is the last visited level $i - 1$ vertex to which v_i is connected. In Figure 6.11 is given the table of d-values for the graph G'' of Figure 6.10.

To associate a portion of the graph G to each node x in a level tree, we consider two ordered sets of vertices $B_1(x)$ and $B_2(x)$. Let x be a node in the tree representing a level i subgraph with $u = b_1(x)$ and $v = b_2(x)$; then $B_1(x) = \langle u, d(u), \ldots, d^{i-1}(u) \rangle$ and $B_2(x) = \langle v, d(v), \ldots, d^{i-1}(v) \rangle$, where $d^{i-1}(u) = \underbrace{d(d(\cdots d(u)))}_{i-1 \text{ times}}$. The associated graph G''_x will be the subgraph containing the vertices in $B_1(x)$ and $B_2(x)$, all vertices encountered in a counterclockwise traversal of level subgraphs starting at $B_1(x)$ and ending at $B_2(x)$. All edges with both endpoints in G_x'' are included, except the ones that leave $B_1(x)$ in a clockwise direction.

To obtain the final tree we have to connect the trees for the different level subgraphs. We construct the whole tree as follows:

Suppose that x is the node corresponding to a face that has inside it a level subgraph with face–face tree T. We connect the tree T as the only child of x. Let y be a leaf of T, $u = b_1(y)$ and $v = b_2(y)$. We consider two cases:

Case 1: $d(u) \neq d(v)$, let z be the first child of x such that $b_1(z) = d(u)$, let z' be the last child of x such that $b_2(z') = d(v)$, if $z \neq z'$ let z'' be the first child of x such that $b_2(z'')$ is connected to v, otherwise $z'' = z'$. We add a new node labeled u as first child of y, the children of u will be all children of x from z to z''. The second child of y when $z' \neq z''$ is a node labeled v that has as children the next children of x before z', and when $z' = z''$ a node labeled $B_2(y)$ that has no child.

When we finally convert the tree into a binary–unary one, a node labeled u will expand into a set of dummy nodes, all of them will keep the same label u.

Case 2: $d(u) = d(v)$, we add two new nodes labeled $B_1(y)$, $B_2(y)$ as first and second children of y.

In Figures 6.12 and 6.13 is given the face–face tree for the graph G'''. Again this construction can be done in $O(\log n)$ parallel time using $O(n^2)$ processors. Thus we get

Lemma 6.3.2 *Given a k-outerplanar graph, we can compute in parallel a face–face tree representation in $O(\log^2 n)$ time and using $O(n^2)$ processors.*

In the previous result, the bounds on the number of processors and on the number of steps are independent of k.

Finally, let us compute the Maximum Independent Set of a given k-outerplanar graph. We consider the face–face tree described in Section 6.2. Recall that by construction, to each node x in a face–face tree we associated two ordered sets of vertices, $B_1(x), B_2(x)$, and a subgraph G_x of the k-outerplanar graph G.

For each node x in the tree with i associated vertices, we compute a table t_x with 2^{i+1} entries $t_x(a, b)$ with $a, b \in \{0, 1\}^i$, each entry contains the

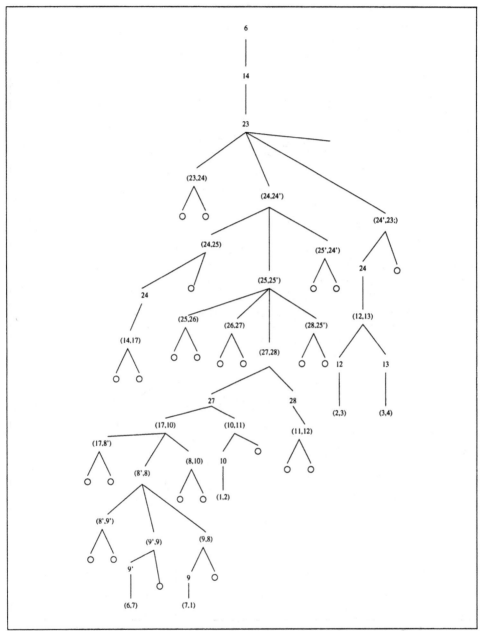

Fig. 6.12: First half of the face–face tree for graph G''

maximum size of an independent set in G_x depending on which of the vertices in $B_1(x)$, or $B_2(x)$ are required to be or not to be in the independent set.

In order to compute tables for the nodes of the face–face tree, we consider three operations on tables: *extension, contraction* and *merging*.

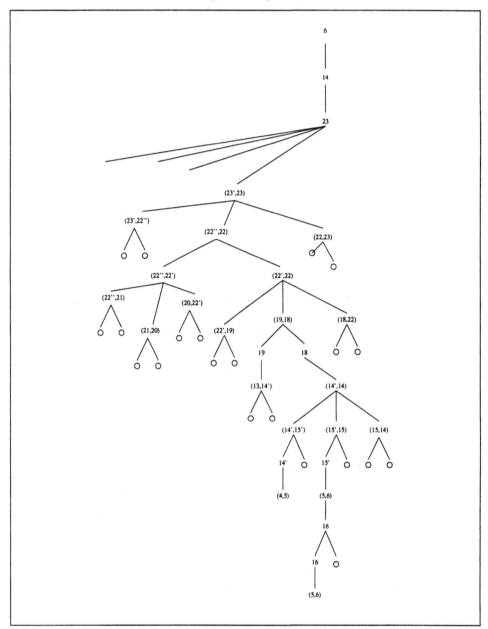

Fig. 6.13: Second half of the face–face tree for graph G''

Given a table for a leaf x on level i, and given a level $i + 1$ node w, we will extend t_x to obtain a table t_{x+w} for a node with associated set of vertices $\langle w, B_1(x)\rangle$, $\langle w, B_2(x)\rangle$. For any of $(a, b) \in \{0, 1\}^i \times \{0, 1\}^i$ representing whether each of the vertices in $B_1(x), B_2(x)$ are required to be in the independent set, the value t_{x+w} will be

$$t_{x+w}(0a, 0b) \;=\; t_x(a, b),$$
$$t_{x+w}(1a, 0b) \;=\; t_{x+w}(0a, 1b) = \text{undefined},$$
$$t_{x+w}(1a, 1b) \;=\; \begin{cases} \text{undefined} & \text{if } w \text{ and a level } i \text{ vertex in the} \\ & \text{independent set are connected,} \\ t_x(a, b) + 1 & \text{otherwise.} \end{cases}$$

In the reverse sense, we define a **table contraction** operation. Given a table for the root of a level i tree, recall that $B_1(x) = \langle w, B'_1(x) \rangle$ and $B_2(x) = \langle w, B'_2(x) \rangle$, we will contract t_x to obtain a table t_{x-w} for a node with associated set of vertices $B'_1(x), B'_2(x)$.

$$t_{x-w}(a, b) = \max\{t_x(0a, 0b), t_x(1a, 1b)\}.$$

We also extend the *merging* operation described in Section 6.2 to deal with sets of more than one vertex, for any $a, b \in \{0, 1\}^i$ ($i \leq k$), let $|c|$ denote the number of 1's in c,

$$t_{xy}(a, b) = \max_{c \in \{0,1\}^i} \{t_x(a, c) + t_y(c, b) - |c|\}.$$

Let us analyze the nodes on the face–face tree corresponding to a k-outerplanar graph. We have two kinds of leaves, all leaves in the level 1 tree are leaves in the tree. The initial table for these leaves will be just the initial tables in the outerplanar case. Other leaves are nodes x labeled by a set of vertices $B(x)$, the initial table is defined as follows: $t_x(a, b)$ will be undefined when $a \neq b$ or when both values are the same but there is an edge between two vertices that have to be included in the independent set, otherwise the value will be the number of 1's in a.

The operation assigned to a non-leaf node x is the following: if x is a node in a level tree that corresponds to a face enclosing a level subgraph, in this case node x has only one unique child and we contract the table for its child. If x is a node labeled u (or v), we extend the table of the left child with u (v) and merge with the table for the right child using the merge operation corresponding to a virtual node. In the rest of the nodes a merging will be performed according to the type of the node.

Note that now the value in each entry of the new table is the size of a Maximum Independent Set including the corresponding vertices, provided that the original tables were correct. Working in a similar way as in Section 6.2 we can define a shunt operation to perform the tree contraction technique.

The merging of tables needs $O(k)$ time and $O(8^k)$ processors. A shunt operation can be done in the same time bounds, but using $O(16^k)$ processors. Thus final computation over the tree needs $O(k \log n)$ time and $O(16^k n)$ processors. Putting together all the bounds we get

Theorem 6.3.3 *There is an* NC *algorithm to solve the* Maximum Independent Set *problem for k-outerplanar graphs running in $O(\log n(k + \log n))$ time and using $O(n(16^k + n))$ processors.*

6.4 The Maximum Independent Set problem for Planar Graphs

The decomposition of a planar graph into k-outerplanar graphs is the same as the one used by Baker ([Bak83], [Bak94]). For each i, $0 \leq i \leq k$, let G_i be the graph obtained by deleting all nodes of G whose levels are congruent to $i \pmod{k+1}$. Now every connected component of G_i is k-outerplanar.

An independent set for G_i can be computed as the union of independent sets for each component. Furthermore, for some r, $0 \leq r \leq k$, the solution for G_r is at least $k/(k+1)$ as large as the optimal solution for G, which follows from the fact that for some r, at most $1/(k+1)$ of the nodes in a Maximum Independent Set for G are at a level that is congruent to $r \pmod{k+1}$. Thus the largest of the solutions for the G_i's is an independent set whose size is at least $k/(k+1)$ optimal, see Algorithm 19.

MAX-INDEP(G)
Given a plane graph G with n nodes.
1 In parallel, compute the associated graph G' and its tree representation.
2 In parallel, make k copies of the tree.
3 For every connected component, in parallel, find the solution to the k-outerplanar graph.
4 For each $0 \leq i \leq k$ add up the sizes of the corresponding components.
5 Compute the maximum over all $i, 0 \leq i \leq k$.

Algorithm 19: NCAS for Max Independent Set on Planar Graphs

Theorem 6.4.1 *Given a plane graph and a constant k, there is an* NC *approximation algorithm to solve the* Maximum Independent Set *problem*

running in time $O(\log n(k + \log n))$, using $O(n^2(16^k + n))$ processors and achieving a solution at least $k/(k + 1)$ optimal. Thus, taking $\epsilon = 1/k$ we get the Maximum Independent Set *problem for planar graphs in* NCAS, *and taking $k = c \log \log n$ the problem is in* NCAS$^\infty$.

This technique can be transformed to obtain approximations for other optimization problems on planar graphs like Minimum Vertex Cover, Minimum Dominating Set, Minimum Edge Dominating Set and Maximum Matching as well as exact NC algorithms for these problems when restricted to k-outerplanar graphs. Adapting the same technique, it is shown in [DST96] that the Minimum Graph Partition problem on k-outerplanar graphs also belongs to the class NC. (The problem for general graphs is NP-complete.)

An interesting open problem is to lower the bounds on the number of processors. It would be an improvement to obtain an optimal NCAS or even an RNCAS algorithm.

7

Further Parallel Approximations

In this chapter we present some problems for which their NC approximations are obtained using other techniques like "step by step" parallelization of their sequential approximation algorithms. This statement does not imply that the PRAM implementation is trivial. In some cases, several tricks must be used to get it. A difference from previous chapters is the fact that we shall also consider "heuristic" algorithms. In the first section we present two positive parallel approximation results for the Minimum Metric Traveling Salesperson problem. We defer the non-parallel approximability results on the Minimum Metric Traveling Salesperson problem until the next chapter. The following section deals with an important problem we already mentioned at the end of Section 4.1; the Bin Packing problem. We present a parallelization to the asymptotic approximation scheme. We finish by giving a state of the art about parallel approximation algorithms for some other problems, where the techniques used do not fit into any of the previous paradigms of parallel approximation, and which present some interesting open problems.

7.1 The Minimum Metric Traveling Salesperson Problem

Let us start by considering an important problem, the Minimum Metric Traveling Salesperson problem (MTSP). It is well known the problem is in APX. There are several heuristics to do the job. The most famous of them is the constant approximation due to Christofides [Chr76]. Moreover the problem is known to be APX-complete [PY93]. Due to the importance of the problem, quite a few heuristics have been developed for the MTSP problem. For instance, the nearest neighbor heuristics, starting at a given vertex, among all the vertices not yet visited, choose as the next vertex the one that is closest to the current vertex. Repeat this until all vertices have been visited and then return to the initial vertex (see for example Section 6.1 of the book by Garey and Johnson [GJ79]).

Kindervater, Lenstra and Shmoys prove that the nearest neighbor heuristic is P-complete; therefore it looks as if it cannot be implemented in NC. They use a clever reduction from the Circuit Value problem [KLS89]. In the same work, they also prove that several other heuristics for the problem are also P-complete, among them the *nearest merge*, the *nearest insertion* and the *farthest insertion* heuristics. However, a few heuristics can be implemented in parallel. Following the lines of Kindervater, Lenstra and Shmoys, we will present the parallel versions of two well known heuristics which approximate the MTSP.

Let us begin with the **spanning tree** heuristic (see for example [PS82]). The matrix $[d_{ij}]$ will represent the distance matrix associated to the input graph G. Algorithm 20 gives the heuristic.

SPAN $(G, [d_{ij}])$
Given an instance $G = (C, E)$, with $[d_{ij}]$.
1 Find a minimum spanning tree T of G under $[d_{ij}]$.
2 Convert it into an Eulerian spanning graph T_e.
3 Find an Euler tour on T_e by skipping the vertices already visited.

Algorithm 20: Spanning tree heuristic for MTSP

Recall that given a tree, its **Eulerian graph** is the multigraph resulting from duplicating its edges. Given as data structure a double linked adjacent list, it is well known how to obtain with an EREW PRAM its Euler graph, using resource bounds $T(n) = O(1)$ and $W(n) = O(n)$ (see Section 3.2 of [JaJ92]). On the other hand, to find a minimum spanning tree and convert it into a spanning graph can be done with a CREW PRAM in $O(\log^2 n)$ parallel steps and using $O(n^2)$ operations (see for example Section 5.2 of [JaJ92]). Therefore Algorithm 20 can be implemented in parallel giving a $\frac{1}{2}$-approximation to the Minimum Metric Traveling Salesperson problem and the problem belongs to the class NCX.

We have already mentioned that the best approximation, Algorithm 21, for the problem is the Christofides algorithm [Chr76].

The main difficulty in parallelizing Algorithm 21 is that it is not known if the problem of finding a Perfect Matching belongs to NC.

The best we know up to now is the RNC algorithm of Mulmuley, Vazirani

CHRISTOFIDES($G, [d_{ij}]$)

Given an instance $G = (C, V), [d_{ij}]$ to the MTSP.

1 Construct a minimum weight spanning tree and a minimum weight perfect matching on the vertices of odd degree in the tree.

2 Construct an Euler tour in the graph obtained in the previous step.

3 Start at a given vertex and traverse the Euler tour skipping the vertices already visited.

Algorithm 21: Christofides approximation to MTSP

and Vazirani [MVV87] that runs in $O(\log^2 n)$ and uses polylog work (see Algorithm 7). Using their algorithm it is easy to parallelize the Christofides algorithm and thus we obtain an RNC approximation for the Minimum Metric Traveling Salesperson problem. To parallelize the above scheme, Kindervater et al. observed that an approximate Minimum Perfect Matching will suffice to get an approximate tour for the Minimum Metric Traveling Salesperson problem. Therefore, they were able to devise an RNC approximation scheme, to get as close as we wish to a 1/2-approximation, for the Minimum Metric Traveling Salesperson problem, this scheme is given as Algorithm 22. Given any graph G with a distance matrix $[d_{ij}]$ associated to its edges, let $d(G) = \sum_{(i,j) \in E} d_{ij}$.

Theorem 7.1.1 *The family* MTSP$_\epsilon$ *of procedures defined by Algorithm 22 is a* $(\frac{1}{2} + \epsilon)$*-RNC approximation scheme for the* Minimum Metric Traveling Salesperson *problem, where each* $\mathcal{A}_\epsilon$ *uses parallel time* $O(\log^2 n)$ *and polylogarithmic work.*

Proof Let us prove first that the above algorithm achieves the performance guarantee of the statement in the theorem. Let C denote the shortest tour and let M' denote a minimum perfect matching on V with edge weights d_{ij}. If $d(T) \leq 3d(M)/2$ then the double minimum spanning tree has weight at most $2d(T) \leq 3d(M) \leq (3/2)d(C)$. Assume that $d(T) > 3d(M)/2$, for each edge $\{i, j\} \notin E, d_{ij} > 2d(T)/3 > d(M)$, therefore $M \subseteq E$. Since for every $\{i, j\} \in E$ we have $\mu \tilde{d}_{ij} \leq d_{ij} \leq \mu \tilde{d}_{ij} + \mu$ we get $d(M) \leq \sum_{\{i,j\} \in M} (\mu \tilde{d}_{ij} + \mu) \leq d(M') + \epsilon d(T) \leq (1/2 + \epsilon) d(C)$, hence $d(T) + d(M) < (3/2 + \epsilon) d(C)$. Therefore one of the Eulerian graphs produced has weight less than $(3/2 + \epsilon) d(C)$.

MTSP$_\epsilon$(G, [d_{ij}])

Given an instance $G = (V, E)$, [d_{ij}] of MSTP and an $\epsilon > 0$.

1 Construct the minimum spanning tree T.
2 Construct its Euler graph T_e.
3 Identify in T the set V of cities with odd degree.
4 Compute $\mu = \epsilon d(T)|V|$ and $E' = \{(i, j)|d_{ij} \leq 2d(T)/3\}$. For every $(i, j) \in E'$, make $\tilde{d}_{ij} = \lfloor d_{ij}/\mu \rfloor$.
5 Using Algorithm 7, find a perfect matching M on $G' = (V, E')$, [$\tilde{d}_{ij}$]. Add the edges of M to T, call it T^*.
6 Compute its Euler graph T_e^*.
7 Compute $d(T_e^*)$ and $d(T_e)$. Choose the one with minimum value.
8 Construct an Eulerian walk, skipping repeated vertices.

Algorithm 22: MTSP in RNCAS

The resource bounds are straightforward if we observe that

$$\max \tilde{d}_{ij} \leq \left\lfloor \frac{2d(T)/3}{2\epsilon d(T)/|V|} \right\rfloor = |V|/3\epsilon = O(n/\epsilon).$$

$\square$

7.2 Bin Packing

The Bin Packing problem requires us to pack n items, each with size in $(0, 1)$, into a minimal number of unit capacity bins. Approximately solving Bin Packing has been approached in two different ways. The first approach looks into heuristics, analyzing their behaviour, and the second one develops approximation schemes for the problem. One example of such heuristics is the **first fit decreasing** heuristic. It considers the items in order of non-increasing size, and places them sequentially in the first bin with enough capacity. The performance of such algorithms has been studied in [Bak85] and [JDU+74].

Fernandez de la Vega and Lueker showed that Bin Packing has an asymptotic approximation scheme, thus placing the problem in PTAS$^\infty$ [FdlVL81]. As we have already mentioned in Chapter 4 a fully asymptotic approximation scheme improving the previous result was developed by Karmarkar and Karp [KK82], placing the problem in FPTAS$^\infty$.

Anderson, Mayr and Warmuth analyzed the parallel approximability of Bin Packing [AMW89]. They show that the first fit decreasing heuristic is P-complete, but they found a parallel heuristic that achieves the same performance bounds. Furthermore they show how to parallelize the approximation scheme given in [FdlVL81].

In this section we will present the positive results results in [AMW89]. Their parallel heuristic for Bin Packing consists of two stages, in the first one big items are packed according to the first fit decreasing rule and in the second one small items are packed in a greedy manner. Thus the algorithm can be seen also as an approximation scheme for the first fit decreasing packing.

Let us start by showing the parallel algorithm to pack big items using the first fit decreasing heuristic. We will represent an instance x as an ordered set of items $x = (x_1, \ldots, x_n)$ such that $1 \geq x_1 \geq \cdots \geq x_n > 0$ and let $\sigma > 0$ be fixed. The algorithm first breaks the list of items into contiguous sublists in such a way that item sizes within any sublists are within a factor of 2. The algorithm is subdivided into phases, packing in phase i the items with size in $(2^{-(i+1)}, 2^{-i}]$, therefore the number of phases is constant.

Notice that in phase i we can ignore all bins with space $2^{-(i+1)}$ or less, by removing those bins we get a sub-sequence of bins called the $(i + 1)$-**projection**. This projection is further subdivided into **runs**. A run is a contiguous segment of bins whose length is maximal subject to two conditions, (1) the available space is non-increasing and (2) there is an integer t, called the **type** of the run, such that the available space in each bin of the run is in the interval $(2^{-(t+1)}, 2^{-t}]$. A contiguous segment satisfying only the first condition is called a **pre-run**.

Algorithm 23 gives in detail the implementation, variable S contains the list of runs, and gets as initial run ρ_0 which consists of n empty bins.

Packing a sublist into a run is achieved by calling two subroutines, FORWARD-PACK and FILL-IN, until no more items fit into bins of the run, or all items in the sublist have been packed. The first routine computes a pré-run and the second one obtains runs from the pre-runs.

The FORWARD-PACK routine (see Algorithm 24) determines the number k of consecutive items at the beginning of the list that will fit into the first bin of the run. Then it determines how many consecutive blocks of k items can be packed into consecutive bins, following first fit decreasing. Finally, in parallel, the blocks of k items are packed into the appropriate number of leading bins in the run, these bins are removed from the run and returned as a pre-run.

The FILL-IN routine packs the smaller items in the space left in the pre-run. It breaks the pre-run into runs. If all bins in the pre-run were actually

```
      FFD–PACK(L, σ)
 1    S := (ρ₀);
 2    i := 0;
 3    while  2⁻ⁱ ≥ σ do
 4        L' := sublist of items in L with sizes ∈ (2⁻⁽ⁱ⁺¹⁾, 2⁻ⁱ];
 5        S' := ();
 6        if L' ≠ ()
 7            then
 8            repeat
 9                ρ := first run of the (i + 1)-projection of S;
10                FORWARD–PACK(ρ, φ);
11                S'' := FILL–IN (φ);
12                remove from runs in S'' bins with less than ε space;
13                append S'' to S';
14            until L' = ();
15            append the unused portion of the (i + 1)-projection
                of S to S';
16            S := S' with the bins not in the (i + 1)-projection
17                of S merged back;
18        i := i + 1
```

Algorithm 23: Packing big items

filled by the forward packing, these runs would be all of type greater than the phase number and, therefore, no more items could be packed into them in phase i. Otherwise, if the pre-run contains a run of type i FILL-IN tries to pack more items into the bin of the run. Due to the constraints on the amount of space left in type i bins and the size of the items, at most one additional item per bin can be packed by FILL-IN. Notice that to compute the packing we can merge the reversal of the list of amounts of space left in the bins of the run with the list of item sizes, taking care that all bins precede all items of the same size. Interpreting the combined list as a string of parentheses, when bins correspond to openings and items to closings, the natural matching of parentheses gives a first fit decreasing packing.

Theorem 7.2.1 *Algorithm* FFD-PACK(L, σ) *runs in time $c_\sigma \log n$ on an $n/\log n$ processor EREW PRAM. The constant c_σ is polynomial in $1/\epsilon$.*

FORWARD–PACK(ρ, φ)

1   **if** $i \leq$ type of ρ
2   **then** $\varphi := \rho$;
3   $L' = (u_1, \ldots, u_l)$;
4   let $s_1 \leq s_2 \leq \cdots \leq s_{|\rho|}$ be the amounts of space
       available in ρ's bins;
5   $k := \max\{j \mid j \leq |L'|$ and $u_1 + \cdots + u_j \leq s_1\}$;
6   let r be minimal subject to
7       $r = \min\{|\rho|, \lceil l/k \rceil\}$ or
8       $(r+1)k < l$ and $u_{rk+1} + \cdots + u_{(r+1)k+1} \leq s_{r+1}$;
9   remove first r bins from ρ and put them into φ;
10 **if** $\rho = ()$ **then** remove ρ from S;
11 in parallel for $j = 1, \ldots, r$ add to the j-th bin in φ items
       $u_{(j-1)k+1} + \cdots + u_{jk}$

Algorithm 24: Forward-packing

Proof To analyze the complexity of FFD-PACK we need a generalization of the concept of a run. A **stacked run** (or an **s-run**) of type j is a run of type j obtained from the $(j+1)$-projection of the list of bins. As a consequence an s-run of type j may be composed of several runs of type j separated, in the original list, by runs of higher types. Therefore the number of runs can be higher than the number of s-runs, but at most by a factor of 2. To every s-run of type j, we assign a weight of 2^{-2j}. The weight of a list of runs is the sum of the weights of all its s-runs.

Consider the effect of forward packing items in phase i into bins of an s-run of type j, $j < i$. The items packed by FORDWARD-PACK are not necessarily a contiguous sublist since some of the items may be used as fill-ins. Assume that enough items are available to fully pack all bins in the s-run. Disregarding fill-in items, the forward packing of the s-run can create at most

$$\frac{2^{-j}}{2^{-(i+1)}} - \frac{2^{-(j+1)}}{2^{-i}} = \frac{3}{2} 2^{i-j}$$

pre-runs which all decompose into runs of type $i + 1$ or higher. Thus the weight of the s-runs resulting from forward packing to capacity one s-runs of type j in phase i is bounded by

$$\frac{3}{2}2^{i-j}\sum_{k>i}2^{-2k} < 2^{-2j}.$$

The forward packing routine may also leave a partially filled bin or fail to pack a whole s-run. Since at most one s-run of every type can be partially packed in this way, this fact adds, for the whole phase, a weight bounded by

$$\sum_{k\geq 0}2^{-2k} = \frac{4}{3}.$$

Now we consider the effect of the FILL-IN routine on the weight of s-runs. In phase i only s-runs of type i will be affected. Assume that when filling an s-run of type i fill-in creates two new s-runs of type $j > i$. Then all items added to the bins in the first s-run come after the items in the second one in the item list. Let $u(v)$ be the size of the fill-in items packed into the first bin of the first (second) new s-run. Since the item of size v came earlier in the item list, it did not fit into the first bin of the first run. After the size u item is packed there is still an amount of space larger than $2^{-(j+1)}$ left, since the s-run is of type j. Hence, $v > u + 2^{-(j+1)}$. Now, every s-run of type j generated by fill-in except the last one accounts for a drop of at least $2^{-(j+1)}$ in item size, as all items in phase i are in $(2^{-(i+1)}, 2^i]$, we have that at most 2^{j-i} s-runs of type j can be created. These new runs cause an additional weight increase bounded above by

$$\sum_{j>i}2^{-2j}2^{j-i} = 2^{-2i}.$$

Let w_i be the total weight of the list of bins at the beginning of phase i. Then $w_{i+1} \leq 2w_i + 7/3$ with $w_0 = 1$, and hence, $w_i = O(2^i)$. As in the ith phase we are only concerned with the $(i + 1)$-projection of the list of bins, each s-run has weight at least 2^{-2i}, and there are at most $2 \cdot 2^{2i}w_i$ runs for the algorithm to pack into. The number of runs in the last phase is therefore $O(1/\sigma^3)$. Since the time requirement of the algorithm is clearly $O(\log n)$ for every run generated, the statement of the theorem follows. □

The parallel heuristic for Bin Packing (given as COMPOSITE, Algorithm 25) consists of two stages. The first packs all items of size at least $1/6$ according to first fit decreasing, and the second uses the remaining small items to fill bins up in a greedy manner.

Notice that chunks in step 2 have total size between $1/24$ and $1/6$, except possibly the last chunk. Since the sizes are at least $1/24$, only a constant number of iterations of step 3 are needed, furthermore each iteration can

COMPOSITE(x)

1 Use FFD-PACK to pack all items with size at least $1/6$.

2 Split the remaining items into chunks. Each item of size at least $1/24$ forms a chunk by itself. Let $s_k = \sum_{1 < j \leq k} u_j$, for each i the set $\{u_k \mid i/12 \leq s_k < (i+1)/12\}$ form a chunk.

3 For all bins filled to less than $5/6$ pick a distinct chunk to add to the bin. Repeat until all bins are filled to at least $5/6$ or there are no remaining items.

4 If there are left over items, let U be its total size. Starting with $\lceil 6U/5 \rceil$ in an iteration, each active bin determines how many bins to its left (including itself) are filled to less than $5/6$, and how many items are currently packed in bins to its right. Compute the largest index such that there are enough items to its right to satisfy the request up to and including the bin given by the index. Bins that are emptied by this process become inactive.

Algorithm 25: The composite packing

be implemented using parallel prefix computation. For step 4 notice that every bin will be filled to at least $5/6$, thus an upper bound to the number of bins is $\lceil 6U/5 \rceil$ and since items have size at least $1/24$ a constant number of iterations are needed. Notice that all the required computations can be implemented using parallel prefix computations again.

Theorem 7.2.2 *The composite packing is within a factor of $11/9$ of the optimal, furthermore it can implemented by an algorithm that runs in time $c_\epsilon \log n$ on an $n/\log n$ processor EREW PRAM. The constant c_ϵ is polynomial in $1/\epsilon$.*

Proof The implementation resources come from Theorem 7.2.1 and the fact that parallel prefix computation can be implemented in these bounds.

For the approximation ratio, let L be the length of the first fit decreasing packing of the items with size at least $1/6$. Clearly L is smaller than the number of bins needed to pack all items using the first fit decreasing heuristic (L_{ffd}). In the case where the second stage of the composite packing needs any additional bin, we know that all bins, except possibly the last one, will be filled to at least 5/6, that is within a 6/5 factor of optimum. Therefore as L_{ffd} is within a factor of 11/9 of optimum we get the desired bound. $\square$

Let us improve a bit the parallel approximation of Bin Packing. The basic techniques used in the algorithm in [FdlVL81] are similar to those used to get approximation schemes:

- Elimination of small items
- Interval partitioning
- Rounding

The schema is an asymptotic result because the performance bounds for the algorithm which runs in linear time satisfy $\mathcal{A}_\epsilon(x) \leq (1 + \epsilon)\,\mathrm{Opt}(x) + 1$, the additive term makes of it an asymptotic approximation scheme. Although the running time is linear in the instance length it is exponential in ϵ. The resulting procedure is given in Algorithm 26.

BIN-PACK(x, ϵ)

1 $\delta := \epsilon/2$.

2 Split x into two lists, y with all items with size at least δ, and z with the remaining items. Let n' be the number of items in y.

3 Call LIN-GROUP with parameter $k = \lceil \frac{\epsilon^2}{2} n' \rceil$. Let y' and y'' be the two sequences of items obtained.

4 Pack y' optimally using Lenstra's algorithm to solve the integer programming formulation of Bin Packing.

5 Pack the k items in y'' into at most k bins.

6 Obtain a packing of y, using the same number of bins, replacing each item in y', y'' by its corresponding item in y.

7 Using First Fit, pack all the small items in z, using new bins only if necessary.

Algorithm 26: Asymptotic PTAS for Bin Packing

The implementation of the LIN-GROUP routine is given in Algorithm 27. Therefore it is easy to see that steps 1–3, 5 and 6 can easily be implemented in parallel. For step 7 a technique similar to the second part of the parallel composite heuristic can be used to finally pack the small items.

A little more care is neeeded to understand the implementation of step 4.

LIN-GROUP(x, k)

1 Let $m = \lfloor n/k \rfloor$ and define the item groups $G_i = \{x_{(i-1)k+1}, \ldots, x_{ik}\}$, for $1 \leq i \leq m$, and let G_{m+1} contain the remainder.

2 For each group G_i obtain a new group of items H_i that has as many items as G_i each of size $x_{(i-1)k+1}$.

3 Construct the Bin Packing instance x' formed by all items in groups $H_2, \ldots, H_{m+1}$.

4 Construct the Bin Packing instance x'' formed by all items in groups H_1.

Algorithm 27: Linear Grouping for Bin Packing

The main purpose of LIN-GROUP is to obtain an instance of Bin Packing that has only a small number of size types, in fact this number is independent of n and therefore constant. Such an instance can be seen as a multiset $M = \{n_1 : \sigma_1, \ldots, n_m : \sigma_m\}$. Furthermore notice all sizes are at least δ. As we have repeated weights we can also express the packing of a unit length bin by an m-vector $B = (b_1, \ldots, b_m)$ giving the number of items of each size. Therefore we can use all vectors corresponding to legal packings, that is $\sum_{i=1}^{n} b_i \sigma_i$. Let the matrix A be a matrix whose rows are formed by all legal bin vectors. The fact that we get a complete packing of the items in M can now be expresed by linear equations that represent the selected bin assignments, therefore Bin Packing can be expresed as

$$\begin{cases} \min \sum_{i=1}^{n} x_i \\ \vec{x} A \geq \vec{\sigma} \\ x_i \in \{0, 1\} \end{cases}$$

Notice that the main point with the above formulation is that first the number of rows in A is exponential in m and δ, in fact it can be bounded by $\binom{m/\delta}{1/\delta}$. But recall that m and δ are independent of n (not of ϵ) and therefore we can construct and solve the above integer programming problem in constant sequential time and therefore in constant parallel time. Therefore Bin Packing is in NCAS$^\infty$.

Theorem 7.2.3 *There is an asymptotic NC approximation scheme for the Bin Packing problem.*

7.3 More Cut Problems

The Minimum k-Cut problem and its variations have been extensively studied. For general graphs the problem is NP-hard [GH88]. For a fixed value of k, the problem is solvable with running time a polynomial of order $O(k)$ in n [GH88]. Saran and Vazirani [SV91] gave two different algorithms to obtain a $(1/(2 - 2/k))$-approximation to the Minimum k-Cut problem. The first one, which they call EFFICIENT, is given as Algorithm 28.

EFFICIENT(G, w)

Given an instance $G = (V, E), |V| = n$ with edge weight function w.

1 For each $e \in E$, pick a minimum weight cut s_e that separates the endpoints of e.

2 Sort these cuts by increasing weights.

3 Use a greedy strategy to pick cuts from the sorted list until their union is a k-cut.

Algorithm 28: Approximation to Minimum k-Cut

It is straightforward to parallelize the last algorithm using a random PRAM. For the first step, call Algorithm 7 m times. Choosing a sufficiently large m we can keep the probability of error small. Step 2 can be done in NC with well known techniques and step 3 can also be done in NC using any parallel connected components algorithm. Therefore, we have the following.

Theorem 7.3.1 *The* Minimum k-Cut *problem belongs to the class* RNCX.

It is worth noticing that using the other algorithm in Saran and Vazirani, called SPLIT, we can find an RNC exact solution to the problem for fixed k. This is the parallel counterpart to the sequential result in [GH88].

An interesting open problem is to remove the randomness from the approximation algorithm. Notice that we use Algorithm 12, to solve a flow problem. This implies that any NC aproximation for the Minimum k-Cut problem should involve a different approach, which does not involve solving the Maximum Flow problem.

This is exactly what happened with another problem, the Global Minimum Cut problem. The first sequential solutions to the Global Minimum Cut and the (s, t)-Minimum Cut problems use results from flow theory (applications of Theorem 4.2.1). Later the sequential results were improved using a new technique called *graph contraction* [NI92]. In the parallel domain, the (s,t)-Minimum Cut problem is P-complete for weighted directed graphs [GSS82], and the Global Minimum Cut problem is also P-complete for the same type of graphs [Kar93]. The (s,t)-Minimum Cut problem is in RNC for weighted and unweighted undirected graphs [Kar93]. There is also a flow approach, to get an RNC algorithm for the unweighted directed and undirected graph, using Algorithm 7, together with a reduction described in [MVV87]. Karger and Motwani have given a nice NC exact algorithm for the Global Minimum Cut problem for weighted undirected graphs [KM94]. They first give an RNC approximation scheme for the problem, based on the *contraction technique*. After they produce a randomized reduction from the Global Minimum Cut problem to its approximation problem, obtaining an RNC exact solution. Finally they derandomize this solution, using a combination of two techniques: *pairwise independence* and *random walks in expanders*. We explained the first technique in Chapter 1. An open problem is to find an (R)NC approximation to the (s,t)-Minimum Cut problem for weighted directed graphs.

Given a weighted graph G, and a set of k terminals, a **multiway cut** is a set of edges whose removal disconnects every pair of terminals. This generalizes the fundamental notion of (s,t)-cut. The Minimum Multiway Cut problem consists in finding a multiway cut with minimum weight. The problem is known to be NP-hard [DJP⁺92]. Garg, Vazirani and Yannakakis give a sequential algorithm to approximate the problem using multicommodity flow [GVY96]. The Multicommodity Flow problem can be solved sequentially in polynomial time, by a reduction to linear programming. But as we will see in the next chapter, to approximate the linear programming problem is P-complete, it therefore looks as if a different approach is needed to approximate or to solve exactly in NC the Multicommodity Flow problem. Awerbuch and Leighton [AL93] give an approximation algorithm for distributive systems, working in polynomial time. The algorithm does not use the linear programming approach. However, it does not seem to be easily adapted to the NC setting. The NC approximation to either the Multicommodity Flow problem or the Multiway Cut problem remains an open question.

7.4 Other Problems

Berger and Shor [BS90] gave a $(1/2 + 1/\sqrt{d_G})$-approximation algorithm for the problem of the Maximum Acyclic Subgraph, where d_G is the maximum degree among all the vertices in G. They gave a direct RNC implementation of their algorithm, and made a comment to the effect that it was possible to derandomize it and thus put it in NCX.

There are many other problems where "direct" parallelization works. For instance Hochbaum and Shmoys [HS86] gave a powerful technique to approximate what they call **bottleneck** problems. These problems comprise a wide variety of NP-complete problems in routing, location and communication network design, among others the Minimum k-center problem, the k-Switching Network problem, the k-Supplier problem, the Metric Bottleneck Traveling Salesperson problem. Their basic technique makes use of two functions: to find Maximal Independent Sets, and Euler tours. Both techniques can be implemented in NC. Therefore, all the algorithms described by Hochbaum and Shmoys could be implemented in NC, and all the problems approximated by their technique are also in NCX.

This field is full of open problems, we have already mentioned a few. In general, a first obvious open question for many problems is the fact that more or less direct translation of the sequential techniques to the parallel ones often does not give the optimal work bound. Therefore, it seems conceivable that a wise use of different techniques could yield better parallel (work–time) bounds.

For some known problems in the class APX nothing is known about their parallel approximability. For instance, the problem of the Shortest Common Superstring is an important problem, with applications in data compression and DNA sequencing. The problem is known to be NP-hard [GJ79]. Blum et al. in [BJL$^+$91] proved that the problem is APX-complete. The best known approximation to the problem is the $\frac{1}{2.89}$-approximation given by Teng and Yao [TY93]. It is an interesting open problem to know if to approximate with a constant the Shortest Common Superstring problem is P-complete or whether it is in NCX. This last possibility would clarify the relationship between the classes APX and NCX.

8

Non-Approximability

In this chapter we consider some problems that are non-approximable by NC algorithms unless P=NC. The basic technique used to prove non-approximability is the design of a reduction that generates instances in such a way that a gap in the value of the objective function is created.

First we concentrate on the Induced Subgraph of High Weight type problems studied in Chapter 3. Anderson and Mayr [AM86] studied this problem when the weight considered is the minimum degree of the graph. They provide a reduction from the Circuit Value problem to the High Degree Subgraph problem that creates a 1/2 gap in the weight of the so obtained instance. Kirousis, Serna and Spirakis studied this problem for two new weight functions, namely, vertex connectivity and edge connectivity, (see [SS89], [Ser90], [KSS93]). Kirousis and Thilikos analyzed the graph linkage [KT96] whose approximability presents the same kind of threshold behavior. All non-approximability results follow the same technique, that is, they create a graph, translating each circuit component or connection into a particular subgraph, in order to generate a graph that satisfies the required gap properties.

Our second result corresponds to problems that are non-approximable in NC, which means that for any ϵ we are able to generate an instance in which an ϵ-gap appears. Serna [Ser91] showed that the linear programming problem cannot be approximated in NC for any ratio, other non-approximable problems can be found in [SS89], [KS88], [Ser90].

To complement the non-approximability view we want to consider also the possible paralellization of heuristics used to deal with NP-hard problems. Each heuristic can be translated into a decision problem that asks for some particular feature of the so obtained solution, in such a way that we can consider the P-completeness of the decision problem. In this context Kindervater, Lenstra and Shmoys analyzed the parallel complexity of several heuristics for the Traveling Salesperson problem showing that some of them are P-complete [KLS89]. Further results on P-completeness of this kind can be found in [AMW89] for Bin Packing.

8.1 The High Connected Subgraph Problem

Recall the definition of the k-Vertex Connected Subgraph problem: Given a graph $G = (V, E)$ and an integer k, does G contain an induced subgraph of vertex connectivity at least k?

The case $k = 3$ for vertex connected induced subgraph is specially interesting. We will show that to test whether a 3-block (a maximal 3-vertex connected subgraph) exists in a graph is P-complete. This must be contrasted with the various algorithms in NC which find all the triconnected (or Tutte, or maximal triply connected) components of a graph. For a definition of 3-blocks see the book by Harary, where they are properly called 3-vertex connected components [Har67]. For the triconnected components, their definition and effects, see for example [ML37], [Tut63] and [MR86].

The Tutte components seem to essentially differ from the 3-blocks because they are defined through a splitting process of the graph, allowing in them chains (of degree 2 vertices), and this helps in a global characterization of them (in NC) as equivalence classes of the transitive closures of certain subgraphs, by an application of Menger's Theorem [Har67]. In contrast 3-blocks (and k-blocks in general) do not allow in them vertices of degree 2 (or virtual edges homeomorphic to actual degree 2 chains). Thus they do not admit a similar global characterization and it is P-complete to test for their existence. Note that to test for the existence of induced subgraphs of high weight seems harder than to test for the existence of induced subgraphs of low weight (the trivial subgraphs could confirm this). However, this is not true in general, the complementary problem to the High Degree Subgraph problem, is the Low Degree Subgraph problem, that consists in finding a maximal induced subgraph of maximum degree at most k. This last problem is NP-complete for several natural decision problems, while for $k = 0$ it corresponds to the Maximal Independent Set problem.

In order to prove that the 3-Vertex Connected Subgraph problem is P-complete, we show first a transformation of an alternating monotone circuit of fan-out 2 into a graph, in the next section we will also show that the so obtained graph satisfies the required properties, that is, it has a 3-vertex (edge) connected subgraph if and only if the circuit outputs **true**.

We consider the following transformation of an alternating monotone cir-

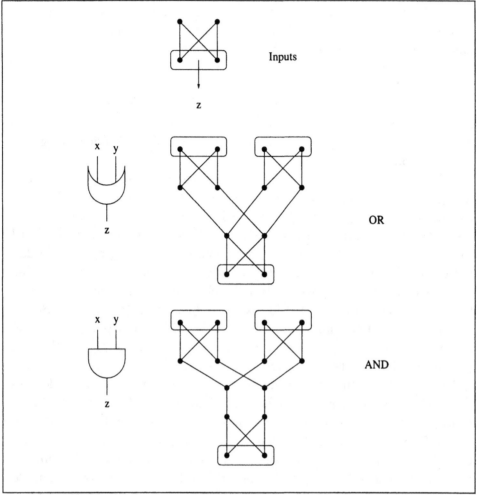

Fig. 8.1: Gadgets to transform inputs, OR and AND gates

cuit A to a graph G_A, the construction can be done in parallel assigning
processors to each input or output node, edge and gate of A.

(i) All input nodes and the output node are replaced by a copy of $K_{2,2}$
(see Figure 8.1).

(ii) Each gate is replaced by the corresponding gadget given in Figure 8.1.

(iii) An edge of the circuit connecting a gate (or input) a to gate (or output) b is replaced by two "parallel edges" that connect the out-nodes
of the gadget of a to the in-nodes of the gadget of b, see Figure 8.2.
Fan-out 2 is allowed by just increasing the degree of the out-nodes of
a, as shown in Figure 8.2.

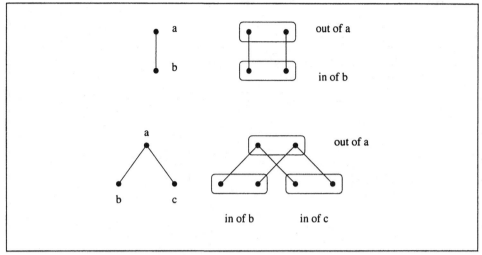

Fig. 8.2: Transformation of wires into edges

(iv) A new extra node is added and this node is connected to the out-nodes of the $K_{2,2}$ graph corresponding to the circuit output node, and to all in-nodes of the value 1 inputs.

In Figures 8.3 and 8.4 are shown a circuit A and the corresponding graph G_A. In this example, for simplicity we omit the "alternating" property of the circuit, which is not actually needed but helps the proof argument.

Lemma 8.1.1 *The above reduction can be done in* NC.

Proof Steps (i) to (iii) are easily performed in constant parallel time. Step (iv) can be performed in $O(\log n)$ parallel time, by assigning a fixed position to the extra node, known by all others processors. □

To prove that the graph G_A has a 3-vertex connected subgraph if and only if A has output value 1 we first define an elimination process which helps the proof.

Given a graph G, we erase all nodes of degree less than 3 and their adjacent nodes. We take a new graph G' as a result, we repeat the above process by setting $G = G'$, untilthe graph contains either only nodes of degree greater than or equal to 3, or no nodes at all.

Lemma 8.1.2 *Given a graph G, if, by application of the elimination process, the whole graph disappears, then G does not contain a 3-vertex connected subgraph.*

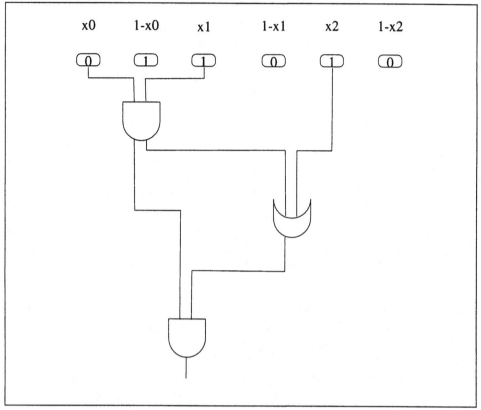

Fig. 8.3: A circuit

Proof Suppose that G contains a 3-vertex connected subgraph. Then no node of degree ≤ 2 can belong to such a subgraph, by definition. Hence, we can eliminate these nodes (thus also the edges adjacent to them) from G. A new graph, G', is then left. Any nontrivial 3-vertex connected subgraph of G would then be a 3-vertex connected subgraph of G', etc. $\square$

Lemma 8.1.3 *If the output of the alternating layered monotone circuit A of fan-out 2 is zero (**false**) then the whole graph G_A will be eliminated by the elimination process, hence G_A cannot contain a 3-vertex connected component.*

Proof To prove the lemma we shall first prove two claims:

Claim 1: All 0-inputs and 0-result gates of G_A will be eliminated by the elimination process.

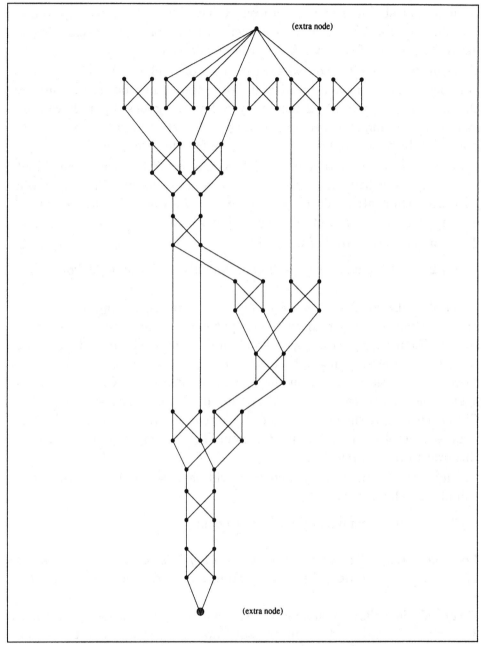

Fig. 8.4: Transformation of the circuit of Figure 8.3

Proof We proceed by induction on the level of the circuit. For $n = 0$ all 0-inputs will be eliminated, just note that such an input has two degree 2 nodes whose removal leaves two other nodes with degree at most 2, due to the fan-out 2 hypothesis (see Figure 8.5).

Assume that all nodes of gates of result 0 have been eliminated, up to and including level k. Let us show that then all nodes of G_A corresponding to gates of result 0 (of the level $k + 1$) will be eliminated.

Consider first the situation where the gates of level $k + 1$ are OR gates. For such a gate to have a result of 0, both inputs must be zeros. Thus by the induction hypothesis all the nodes feeding the gate's inputs have been eliminated. A simple inspection (see Figure 8.5) shows that the whole gate graph will be eliminated as well, due to the fan-out 2 hypothesis.

Now, consider the situation of an AND gate of result 0. At least one input of such a gate will be zero, hence the nodes of G_A feeding that input will have been eliminated. Then (see Figure 8.5) the whole AND gate will be eliminated as well, due to the fan-out 2 hypothesis.

This completes the proof of Claim 1.   □

Claim 2: All 1-inputs and 1-result gates will also be eliminated from G_A.

Proof We will describe a "reserve elimination" process, arguing by induction on the distance of a gate from the output gate of the circuit. First, note that by Claim 1, the output gate graph of G_A will be eliminated. Let k be the maximum level number at which there are gates of result 1. The nodes to which these gates give input have been eliminated, by Claim 1. Let us again consider the cases of an AND gate and an OR gate separately. In Figure 8.6 we give the elimination order for each such gate. Thus, all result 1 gates of level k will be eliminated from G_A. A simple induction carries this over to the 1-inputs.

Finally the extra node will be left (and will have degree 0); thus this node will also be eliminated.   □

    Claims 1 and 2 complete the proof of Lemma 8.1.3   □

Lemma 8.1.4 *If the output of the alternating layered monotone circuit A of fan-out 2 is 1 (**true**), then G_A contains a 3-vertex connected subgraph.*

Proof We define first a subgraph of G_A and then we shall prove that it is 3-vertex connected. Let T_A be the subgraph induced by the set of nodes containing:

  (a) The extra node added to the graph.
  (b) All nodes in paths which start from an in-node of an input with value 1 and end at an out-node of the output of the circuit and pass through nodes of gates with result 1.

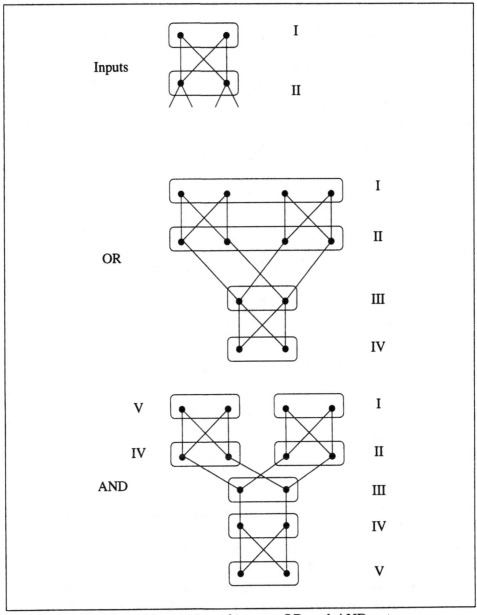

Fig. 8.5: Elimination of inputs, OR and AND gates

Let us prove that T_A is 3-vertex connected. First notice that T_A contains all the nodes of an AND gate with result 1. And for an OR gate, T_A may contain only one of the two incoming branches (the one that corresponds to an incoming value 1).

Assume for sake of contradiction that T_A is not 3-vertex connected. Then

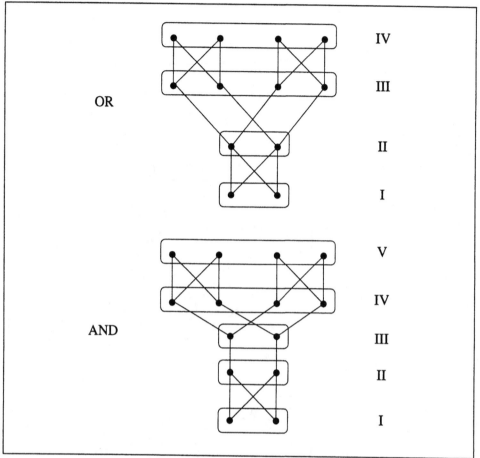

Fig. 8.6: Backward elimination process

there must exist two nodes u, v in T_A whose removal results in T_A being a disconnected or trivial graph. We shall consider three cases:

Case 1: One of u, v (say u) is the extra node. In such a case, if we remove u, T_A will be connected only through the circuit connections. But all those connections consist of "parallel", communicating paths, and all nodes are of degree 2 or more. Hence the removal of any single node cannot disconnect T_A. Thus v cannot exist.

Case 2: Both u, v are in the same gate. Since the in-nodes and out-nodes of the gate connect between them through the extra node, the removal of u and v must leave a piece of the gate disconnected. All the internal nodes in a gate are of degree 3, thus they cannot be isolated by removal of two nodes. The same is true for groups of gate nodes (by exhaustive search, easily seen). Thus, u, v cannot exist.

Case 3: u, v are in different gates or inputs. If they are in gates of the same level then the removal of each of them cannot disconnect the graph. Thus, the interesting case is when u, v are in the same path from an input to an output. But then the existence of the $K_{2,2}$ subgraphs does not allow a disconnection to take place.

This completes the proof of Lemma 8.1.4. □

Lemma 8.1.3 and 8.1.4, together with the above reduction, show that we have the following.

Theorem 8.1.5 *The* 3-Vertex Connected Subgraph *problem is complete for* P *under* NC *reductions.*

Since the testing of whether a graph G contains a k-block (or a k-edge connected induced subgraph) is P-complete for $k \geq 3$, we obtain a first non-approximability result for the High Vertex Connected Subgraph problem using Theorem 2.7.6, namely, "there is no NC approximation algorithm for the optimization version of the k-vertex (edge) connected subgraph with absolute performance ratio less than or equal to 1/4". We will prove that, unless P = NC, no such approximations exist in NC to within a factor ϵ for any $\epsilon > 1/2$. On the approximability side, we have shown approximations in NC to within a factor ϵ, for any $\epsilon < 1/2$ for vertex connectivity. To show the non-approximability of the High Vertex Connected Subgraph to within a 1/2 factor we construct a reduction from the alternating monotone Circuit Value problem to the High Vertex Connected Subgraph problem, the reduction follows the same lines as the one given for the 3-Vertex Connected Subgraph.

Theorem 8.1.6 *Given a graph G, it is not possible to approximate in* NC *the* High Vertex Connected Subgraph *problem for G by a factor $\epsilon > 1/2$ unless* P = NC.

Proof Let $HVCS(G)$ denote the greatest High Vertex Connected Subgraph in G. We will provide an NC transformation of an alternating monotone circuit A to a graph G, such that when the circuit outputs 1, $HVCS(G) = 2k$, and when the circuit outputs 0, $HVCS(G) < k + 1$, that is we will construct a $\frac{1}{2}$-gap reduction from the Circuit Value problem to the High Vertex Connected Subgraph problem. The reduction follows the same lines as those for the 3-Vertex Connected Subgraph problem, we have to define gadgets for each circuit component. We consider the following:

The inputs correspond to k isolated vertices. The OR gate is the gadget

of Figure 8.7, where the boxes represent cliques of numbers of vertices equal
to the number in the box, and circles represent as many isolated vertices as
the number in the circle. In the figure an edge with a label on it actually
means as many edges as the label indicates. Boxes are connected to vertices
in the central circle so that all vertices in a box finally have degree $2k$ and
all vertices in the circle have degree at most $4k - 2$.

The AND gate is the gadget in Figure 8.7, it is obtained from the OR
gate gadget by deleting the edges of the top vertex. Now gate inputs and
outputs correspond to sets of k vertices, for each side, the two distinguished
vertices and $k - 2$ vertices of the corresponding box. Each wire is simulated
by k vertices connected by all possible edges to the two input/output sets
of k vertices.

The output of the final gate, the circuit output, is connected to all vertices
associated to 1-inputs.

The proof is similar to those of Lemmas 8.1.3 and 8.1.4, we have that,
when the output of the circuit is 1, then the subset of the 1-inputs and
the gates with output 1 which lead to the final gate define a $2k$-vertex
connected subgraph. But, when the circuit outputs 0, the minimum degree
of any induced subgraph of the graph is at most $k + 1$, thus it cannot have
a $k + 1$ connected subgraph.   □

8.2 Linear Programming

Since, as we show later on, the parallel complexity of linear programming
does not depend on the size of the numbers involved, that is linear programming is P-complete in the strong sense, we have no hope of restricting the
size of numbers and having a subproblem in NC. Another possible restriction to consider concerns the number of variables per inequality, but even
the simplest linear programming problem with two variables per inequality
is P-complete (see [LMR86]).

Looking at the definition of the Linear Programming problem, we can
consider two approximation problems. The first one is an approximation on
the solution space, that is trying to obtain a vector near to the solution in
some suitable norm, independently of the value of the objective function on
it. The second is an approximation on the objective function space, trying
to compute a vector that may or may not be near to a solution, but such
that the objective function on it attains a value close to the optimal value.

We will show that both of these approximation problems cannot be solved
in NC, unless P $=$ NC, showing that the problem of computing an ϵ-
approximations is a P-complete problem for any ϵ. In order to obtain the

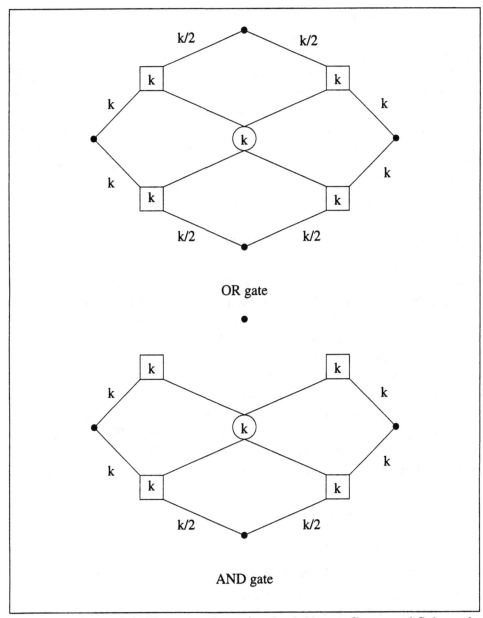

Fig. 8.7: OR and AND gate gadgets for the k-Vertex Connected Subgraph problem

above result we introduce first the True Gates problem, this problem takes as input an encoding of a boolean circuit, and outputs the number of gates such that their output value is **true**. Once we prove the non-approximability of the True Gates problem, we translate the result to the linear programming problem, constructing an NC reduction which transforms a boolean circuit into a lpinear programming instance and preserves the value of the corresponding optimal solutions.

Given an encoding of a boolean circuit A, we denote by $TG(A)$ the number of gates such that their output value is 1 (**true**). We consider the problem of the Circuit True Gates problem given an encoding of a boolean circuit A, compute $TG(A)$. Given a circuit, let ϵ-CTGP denote the problem of finding an ϵ-approximation to the value of the Circuit True Gates problem. We use the Circuit Value problem, to prove the non-approximability of ϵ-CTGP. The technique used here follows the traditional way of defining an NC reduction which creates a gap on the function considered.

Theorem 8.2.1 *The ϵ-CTGP is P-complete for any $\epsilon \in (0, 1]$.*

Proof First notice that ϵ-CTGP is trivially in P. We now reduce the Circuit Value problem to ϵ-CTGP. We provide a log-space transformation of a circuit A on n gates to a bigger circuit A' such that if the output of A is 1, then in A' the number of true gates is greater than $\lceil n/\epsilon \rceil$ and if the output of A is 0, then this number is less than n. Thus, if we had an algorithm in NC to approximate $TG(A')$ within a factor ϵ, then we would get an algorithm in NC that would decide the output of A.

Let $A = (\alpha_1, \dots, \alpha_n)$ and let $l = \lceil n/\epsilon \rceil$, the new circuit is obtained from A by adding l gates, these gates will alternate between AND an OR, propagating in a trivial way the output value of circuit A. The construction is suggested in Figure 8.8; formally, we define $A' = (\alpha_1, \dots, \alpha_n, \alpha_{n+1}, \dots, \alpha_{n+l})$, where

$$\alpha_{n+k} = \alpha_{n+k-1} \wedge \alpha_{n+k-1} \qquad \text{for} \qquad k = 1, 3, \dots,$$

$$\alpha_{n+k} = \alpha_{n+k-1} \vee \alpha_{n+k-1} \qquad \text{for} \qquad k = 2, 4, \dots.$$

As the circuit added to A only propagates A's output, we have

(a) If the circuit A outputs 0 then
$TG(A') = TG(A) < n,$
(b) If the circuit A outputs 1 then
$TG(A') = TG(A) + l \geq \lceil \frac{n}{\epsilon} \rceil.$

$\square$

Note that the circuit given in Figure 8.8 is planar and alternating, further all gates have fan-in 2 and fan-out 2. So, using whatever kind of circuits which follow the above restrictions, the reduction described in Theorem 8.2.1

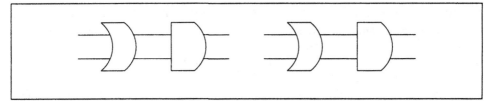

Fig. 8.8: Alternating propagator

provides a log-space reduction from the specific circuit value problem to the corresponding ϵ-true gates problem, then we have

Theorem 8.2.2 *The ϵ-CTGP is P-complete for any $\epsilon \in (0,1]$, for any of the following circuit classes: binary, monotone, fan-out 2 monotone, planar, alternating and fan-out 2 alternating.*

Let us first define formally the Linear Inequalities and the linear programming problems.

The Linear Inequalities problem consists in, given an integer $n \times d$ matrix A, and an integer n-vector b, deciding if there is a rational d-vector x such that $Ax \leq b$, while the linear programming problem also has a linear function to optimize.

Theorem 8.2.3 (Dobkin, Lipton, Reiss, Khachian) *The* Linear Inequalities *and the* linear programming *problems are complete for the class* P.

In order to obtain easily the strong P-completeness result, we start by giving a direct reduction from the Circuit Value problem to the Linear Inequalities problem.

Given an encoding of a boolean circuit A, we construct an instance of the Linear Inequalities problem as follows:

(1) We generate the inequalities $x_k \leq 1$ and $x_k \geq 0$ for $0 \leq k \leq n$.
(2) If α_k is a 0-input gate generate the equation $x_0 = 0$, and if it is a 1-input gate generate $x_1 = 1$.
(3) If $\alpha_k = \neg \alpha_j$ generate the equation $x_k = 1 - x_j$.
(4) If $\alpha_k = \alpha_i \wedge \alpha_j$ generate the inequalities $x_k \leq x_i$, $x_k \leq x_j$ and $x_i + x_j - 1 \leq x_k$.
(5) If $\alpha_k = \alpha_i \vee \alpha_j$ generate the inequalities $x_i \leq x_k$, $x_j \leq x_k$ and $x_k \leq x_i + x_j$.

Clearly, the transformation can be done in log-space, further we have

Lemma 8.2.4 *The solution of the instance to the* linear programming *problem constructed above satisfies*

$$x_i = 1 \ \textit{iff} \ \alpha_i \ \textit{outputs } 1.$$

Proof Note that considering the set of inequalities obtained in steps (1) to (5), we have, for any gate, if the inputs are 0 or 1 then the output (in the system) will be 0 or 1, according to the corresponding boolean function. Thus, the unique solution of this subsystem satisfies $x_i = 1$ iff α_i has value 1.   □

Using the above lemma the transformation can be easily adapted to give a reduction from the Circuit Value problem to the Linear Inequalities problem, just add step (6) $x_n = 0$, or the linear programming problem, add step (6) $c_i = 0$, $i = 1, \dots, n-1$ and $c_n = 1$. Both reductions satisfy the condition that all the coefficients of the so obtained instance for the Linear Programming (Linear Inequalities) problem have value 0 or 1, so we immediately can state

Theorem 8.2.5 *The* Linear Inequalities *and the* Linear Programming *problems are*P*-complete in the strong sense.*

Let x_0 be the exact solution to a linear programming instance, and x an approximate solution, we distinguish between two types of approximations. A **solution approximation** requires an x close to x_0 in some suitable norm. A **value approximation** requires only $c^T x$ close to $c^T x_0$. Actually, we have dropped, for approximate solutions, the condition "satisfy all the inequalities simultaneously". Formally, for any particular $\epsilon \in (0, 1]$ we consider the following approximation problems.

The Solution Approximation problem to linear programming (ϵ-LPS) consists in computing x such that

$$||x_0||_p \geq ||x||_p \geq \epsilon \, ||x_0||_p$$

where $||x||_p = (\sum_{i=1}^{d} x_i^p)^{1/p}$. The problem of ($\epsilon$-LPV) consists in computing x such that

$$c^T x_0 \geq c^T x \geq \epsilon \, c^T x_0.$$

We will show that both approximation problems are P-complete for any value of ϵ. In order to show this result, we use the negative approximability results obtained, in Theorem 8.2.1, for the problem of computing the number of true gates in a boolean circuit. We first provide a log-space transformation from a boolean circuit A to an instance of the linear programming problem. The transformation is a slight modification of the one used in Lemma 8.2.4.

(1)–(5) as in Lemma 8.2.4,
    (6) $c_i = 1$, for all i.

Lemma 8.2.6 *The solution to the instance constructed above for the* linear *programming* is the number of true gates in the circuit A.

Proof From Lemma 8.2.4 the unique solution of the system satisfies $x_i = 1$ if and only if α_i has value 1. So the equation in step 6 has a unique possible solution and it is the number of true gates. $\square$

The above transformation gives us a reduction from the Circuit Value problem to the linear programming problem, in such a way that the maximum possible value attained by the objective function is just the number of true gates, extending this property to the p-norm of solutions we have the desired result.

Theorem 8.2.7 *The following hold.*

    (i) *The ϵ-LPV problem is complete for the class* P *under log-space reductions for any $\epsilon \in (0, 1]$.*
    (ii) *The ϵ-LPS problem is complete for the class* P *under log-space reductions for any $\epsilon \in (0, 1]$ and any $p \geq 1$.*

Proof We consider the transformation given above, from Lemma 8.2.4 we have that the solution x of the linear programming instance is a $0/1$ vector, then we have

$$||x||_p = (\sum_{i=1}^{d} x_i^p)^{1/p} = ||x||_1 = TG(A) \text{ for all } p \geq 1.$$

Thus, any ϵ-approximation to LPS or LPV becomes an ϵ-approximation to the Circuit True Gates problem. $\square$

Finally, using Theorem 2.7.4 we have

Theorem 8.2.8 *The linear programming* problem cannot have an NC *approximation algorithm A with $R_A < \infty$.*

As a corollary to this theorem, we get

Theorem 8.2.9 *We have* P $=$ NP *if and only if we have* APX $=$ NCX.

8.3 The Nearest Neighbor Heuristic

One of the heuristics used to deal with the Minimum Metric Traveling Sales-person problem is the so called *nearest neighbor tour*. The nearest neighbor heuristic is given as Algorithm 29.

NNT(G)
1 Start at a given vertex.
2 Among all vertices not yet visited, choose as the next vertex the one that is closest to the current vertex. Repeat this step until all vertices have been visited.
3 Return to the starting vertex.

Algorithm 29: Nearest neighbor algorithm

For the nearest neighbor heuristic we consider the following associated problem:

Given a distance matrix $[d_{i,j}]$ and two vertices v_1 and v_2, does the nearest neighbor tour starting at vertex v_1 visit vertex v_2 as the last one before returning to vertex v_1?

We will show that the above problem is P-complete, to do so we construct a reduction for the Circuit Value problem for circuits formed by fan-out 2 NAND gates. Each gate of the circuit will be replaced by a subgraph. The nearest neighbor tour will visit gates in the same order that they have in the circuit. This will insure that when the tour visits a gate it has already visited both inputs.

We will transform a circuit with m NAND gates and n inputs into a weighted graph. The gadget for the kth NAND gate is given in Figure 8.9. The vertex pairs 1–2 are shared by different subgraphs, if gate i is input to gate k the vertices in a 1–2 output pair of gate i and one 1–2 input pair are the same vertices. The edge weight 0 insures that both vertices are always neighbors in the tour. When the gate has fan-out 1 we use the same gadget, but with only a 1–2 output pair.

The subgraph is constructed in such a way that if the nearest neighbor tour enters the subgraph at vertex A from subgraph $k-1$ it leaves through vertex B to subgraph $k+1$. But in going from A to B there are three possible ways. Notice that if both 1–2 pairs of input vertices are not yet visited (or only one of them) the tour will pass through them before reaching B. Thus it will

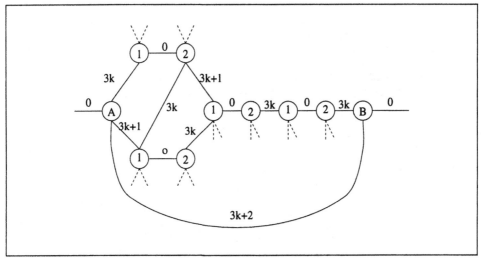

Fig. 8.9: The graph for NAND gate k

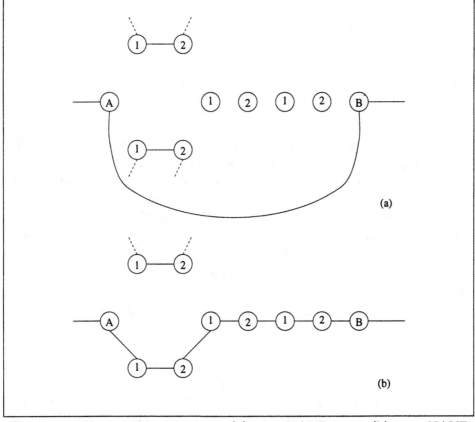

Fig. 8.10: The possible situations: (a) **true** NAND **true**; (b) **true** NAND **false**.

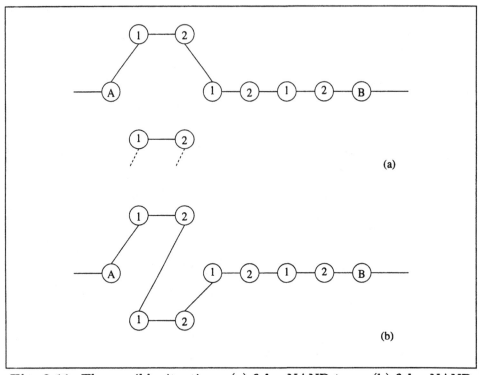

Fig. 8.11: The possible situations: (a) **false** NAND **true**; (b) **false** NAND **false**.

take the direct connection from A to B only when both inputs have already been visited. Notice that in the first case the tour will also pass through the output nodes, while in the second case it will not (see Figures 8.10 and 8.11). Note that in all cases all unvisited input vertices are included in the tour.

Now we only need to associate with a subgraph the value **true** (**false**) if the nearest neighbor tour passes (does not pass) through the output vertices, to obtain a circuit simulation. Recall that if both inputs are visited that implies that when traversing the input subgraph it passes through the output nodes, that is two **true** inputs, and then the output is **false**. In the other case one of the inputs is **false** and that implies that some input vertices are yet unvisited, so the tour will now cover the output vertices, but that is just output **true**.

For **true** and **false** inputs we construct the subgraphs shown in Figure 8.12. The subgraph corresponding to input 1 is a special case. Instead of the length 0 edge, it has two edges of length $3m+3$ which connect it to the subgraph corresponding to the last NAND gate m. Also the representation of the last gate has some special features. In it the output vertices have been

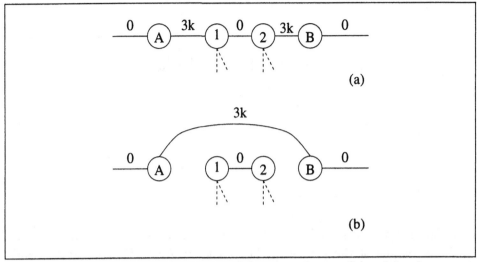

Fig. 8.12: The graph for inputs, (a) a **true** input; (b) a **false** input.

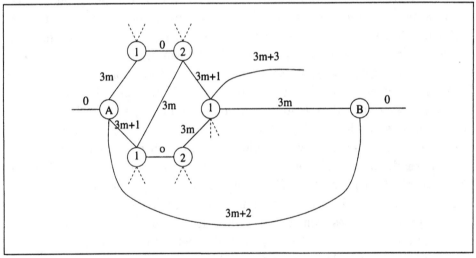

Fig. 8.13: The graph gadget of the last gate

replaced by a single vertex C, and both vertices B and C are connected to the first input gadget (see Figure 8.13).

It should be clear now that a nearest neighbor tour starting at the vertex A of the first input visits the vertex B of the last gate if and only if the circuit outputs **true**. Since the transformation can be performed in NC we have

Theorem 8.3.1 *A nearest neighbor tour of a given graph cannot be computed in* NC *unless* P = NC.

9

Syntactically Defined Classes

In Chapter 2, we presented several complexity classes based on the approximability degree of the problems they contain: APX, PTAS, FPTAS and their parallel counterparts NCX, NCAS, FNCAS. These classes, defined in terms of degree of approximability, are known as the "computationally defined" approximation classes. We have seen that in order to show that a problem belongs to one of these classes, one can present an approximation algorithm or a reduction to a problem with known approximability properties. In this chapter we show that in some cases the approximation properties of a problem can be obtained directly from its syntactical definition. These results are based on Fagin's characterization of the class NP in terms of existential second-order logic [Fag75], which constitutes one of the most interesting connections between logic and complexity. Papadimitriou and Yannakakis discovered that Fagin's characterization can be adapted to deal with optimization problems. They defined classes of approximation problems according to their syntactical characterization [PY91]. The importance of this approach comes from the fact that approximation properties of the optimization problems can be derived from their characterization in terms of logical quantifiers. Papadimitriou and Yannakakis defined the complexity classes MaxSNP and MaxNP which contain optimization versions of many important NP problems. They showed that many MaxSNP problems are in fact complete for the class. The paradigmatic MaxSNP-complete problem is Maximum 3SAT. Recall that the Maximum 3SAT problem consists in, given a boolean formula F written in conjunctive normal form with three literals in each clause, finding a truth assignment that satisfies the maximum number of clauses. For the case of MaxNP, Papadimitriou and Yannakakis did not find a complete problem, but showed that the Maximum GSAT(B) problem lies in the class and every problem in MaxNP can be reduced to the Maximum GSAT(B) problem for some constant B. The Maximum GSAT(B)

problem consists in, given a conjunction of subformulas $F_1, \ldots, F_m$ where each F_i is a disjunction of implicants (conjunctions of literals) and each implicant contains up to B literals, finding a truth assignment that satisfies the maximum number of subformulas. This result, as well as the completeness of Maximum 3SAT, was originally proved for L-reductions but they also hold for the log-space E-reduction.

Later it was also proved that the closures under polynomial time E-reduction of MaxSNP and MaxNP coincide, and therefore Maximum 3SAT is also MaxNP-complete under poly E-reduction [KMSV94] (such a result for the log-space E-reduction is not known).

Papadimitriou and Yannakakis also proved that all the problems in the classes MaxSNP and MaxNP have polynomial time (constant factor) approximation algorithms, thus showing that both classes are contained in the class APX. In this chapter we show that in fact all the problems in MaxSNP and MaxNP have parallel approximation algorithms and therefore both classes are contained in NCX.

From the result by Arora et al. [ALM+92] it follows that for every problem that is hard for MaxSNP there is a constant c such that the problem cannot be approximated in polynomial time by a factor smaller than c (unless P = NP). This implies obviously that under the hypothesis P $\neq$ NP, the problem cannot be approximated in NC by a factor smaller than c. We present a result showing that for every problem in MaxSNP there is also a constant c' such that the problem cannot be approximated by a factor smaller than c' unless NC = P [SX95].

9.1 MaxNP and MaxSNP

Let us start by defining the classes MaxSNP and MaxNP; for this definition we need to consider first the syntactic versions of the classes. They define a class of optimization problems that admit the following syntactic characterization as maximization problem over logical quantifiers.

Definition 9.1.1 Syntactic MaxSNP *is the class of NPO problems* Π *that can be expressed in the form*

$$\text{Opt}_\Pi(x) = \max_s |\{\overline{y} : \varphi_\Pi(x, s, \overline{y})\}|$$

where φ_Π *is a quantifier free formula,* x *is an instance of the input problem* Π *described as a finite structure, and* s *is a solution of instance* x.

The optimization problem seeks for a solution $s \in D(i)$ maximizing the number of tuples $\bar{x}$ for which φ_Π holds. We observe that the problem Maximum 3SAT admits such a characterization.

Lemma 9.1.1 Maximum 3SAT *is in* MaxSNP.

Proof We consider four input relations F_0, F_1, F_2 and F_3 that express the clauses of F with 0, 1, 2 and 3 negative literals. $F_0(x, y, z)$, $F_1(x, y, z)$, $F_2(x, y, z)$ and $F_3(x, y, z)$ are true if and only if $(x \vee y \vee z)$, $(\neg x \vee y \vee z)$, $(\neg x \vee \neg y \vee z)$ and $(\neg x \vee \neg y \vee \neg z)$ respectively is the jth clause of F. (We suppose that in each clause the negated variables are written first, and they are lexicographically ordered). We also consider the relation S that assigns to every variable of the formula value **true** or **false**. We can define

$$\begin{aligned}
\varphi(F, S, x, y, z, j) =& (F_0(x, y, z, j) \wedge (S(x) \vee S(y) \vee S(z))) \\
& \vee (F_1(x, y, z, j) \wedge (\neg S(x) \vee S(y) \vee S(z))) \\
& \vee (F_2(x, y, z, j) \wedge (\neg S(x) \vee \neg S(y) \vee S(z))) \\
& \vee (F_3(x, y, z, j) \wedge (\neg S(x) \vee \neg S(y) \vee \neg S(z))).
\end{aligned}$$

The assignment S maximizing the number of simultaneously satisfiable clauses is $\max_S |\{(x, y, z, j)|\varphi(F, S, x, y, z, j)\}|$.   □

Another important problem in the class Syntactic MaxSNP is the Maximum Cut.

Analogously Syntactic MaxNP is defined as follows.

Definition 9.1.2 Syntactic MaxNP *is the class of* NP *optimization problems* Π *that can be expressed in the form*

$$\mathrm{Opt}_\Pi(i) = \max_s |\{\bar{x}|\exists \bar{y} \varphi_\Pi(i, s, \bar{x}, \bar{y})\}|$$

where φ_Π *is a quantifier free formula,* i *is an instance of the input problem* Π *described as a finite structure, and* $s \in D(i)$ *is a solution of the problem.*

The definitions of these classes express syntactic properties of the optimization problems being considered, and therefore they do not provide us with a very robust concept. It can be the case that a problem belongs to one of the classes when encoded in a certain way, but does not belong under a different encoding. In order to make the classes more robust and to be able to define in a syntactic manner classes that capture all the problems with a

specified approximability, as in the computationally defined classes, the closures under approximation preserving reductions of the syntactically defined
classes have been considered. Recall that the **closure** of a class C under a
given structure preserving reduction is the set of all NPO problems that are
reducible to some problem in C. Papadimitriou and Yannakakis considered
the closure of the syntactic classes under the L-reduction. Khanna et al.
[KMSV94] have proved that the closures of Syntactic MaxSNP and Syntactic MaxNP under polynomial time E-reduction are the same and coincide
exactly with APX.

We consider here the closure of these classes under the log-space E-
reduction.

Definition 9.1.3 *The classes* **MaxSNP** *and* **MaxNP** *are the closures
of the classes* Syntactic MaxSNP *and* Syntactic MaxNP *under logarithmic
space E-reduction.*

In the way MaxSNP and MaxNP are defined here, these classes contain the
closure of the syntactic classes under log-space L-reductions. As we showed
in the introduction, the Maximum Satisfiability problem can be trivially
approximated within NC. The same algorithm works for Maximum 3SAT,
and therefore this problem belongs to NCX. For any fixed value B, the
problem Max GSAT(B) can also be approximated in NC within a constant
factor.

Proposition 9.1.2 *The* Max GSAT(B)*problem can be approximated with
constant factor in* NC.

Proof Let F be a formula with n variables defined by the conjunction of m
subformulas $F_1, \ldots, F_m$, where each F_i is a disjunction of implicants, and
each implicant contains at most B literals. Let S denote an assignment and
$X(F_i, S)$ $1 \leq i \leq m$, be the variables

$$X(F_i, S) = \begin{cases} 1 & \text{if } S \text{ satisfies the subformula } F_i, \\ 0 & \text{otherwise.} \end{cases}$$

Consider also the function m denoting the number of subformulas that are
satisfied by S,

$$m(S) := \sum_{i=1}^{m} X(F_i, S)$$

and let us estimate the expected value $E[m(S)]$ under the uniform distribution of the assignments. First we have that $E[X(F_i, S)] = \Pr[S \text{ satisfies } F_i]$

where F_i is a disjunction of implicants containing at most B literals and each of these implicants is satisfied by at least 2^{n-B} assignments. It follows that

$$Pr[S \text{ satisfies } F_i] \geq \frac{2^{n-B}}{2^n} = 2^{-B}.$$

$$E[m(S)] = E[\sum_{i=1}^{m} X(F_i, S)] = \sum_{i=1}^{m} E[X(F_i, S)] \geq m2^{-B}.$$

On the average a randomly selected assignment would satisfy a 2^{-B} fraction of the total number of subformulas. It is not hard to see that for the above estimation of the expected value of $m(S)$ it is not needed that the literals are chosen totally independently; B-wise independence suffices. Because of this fact, we can use derandomization techniques from [Lub86], and define a probability distribution on the set of assignments for a formula F, with the properties that there are only a polynomial number of assignments with non-zero probability, and that the expected value of $m(S)$ under the new distribution coincides with $E[m(S)]$ under the uniform distribution. All these (polynomially many) assignments can be computed in parallel, and the approximation algorithm selects the one that satisfies the most subformulas. Since $E(m(S)) \geq m2^{-B}$, the assignment selected by the algorithm satisfies at least $\frac{m}{2^B}$ subformulas which proves that Max GSAT(B) can be approximated in NC with constant relative approximation error $2^B - 1$.   □

The parallel approximation properties of Max GSAT(B) hold for every problem in MaxNP since every problem in this class can be log-space E-reduced to a Max GSAT(B) problem for a particular value of B, and E-reductions preserve approximability. From the previous argument, we can conclude that the following holds.

Theorem 9.1.3 *The class* MaxNP *is contained in the class* NCX.

As we have mentioned, Khanna et al.   [KMSV94] have proved that the closures under polynomial time E-reduction of the syntactic classes MaxSNP and MaxNP coincide exactly with the computationally defined class APX. An interesting open problem is to derive a similar connection for the parallel case, studying whether it is possible to define a fine grain reduction in NC, such that the closures of Syntactic MaxSNP and MaxNP under that reduction coincide with the class NCX.

9.2 Limits for the Approximation

We have shown that MaxSNP is included in NCX, and therefore every problem in the class can be approximated in NC for some constant factor c. We show next that these approximations cannot be arbitrarily improved, presenting a result from Serna and Xhafa [SX95] that proves that for every problem that is MaxSNP-hard there is also a constant c' such that the problem cannot be approximated by a factor smaller than c' unless P = NC. Consider the concept of **local search algorithms** [JPY88], a general approach when dealing with hard optimization problems. Starting from an initial solution, the algorithm moves to a better one among its neighbors, until a *locally optimal* solution is found. *Non-oblivious local search*, a variant of the classical local search algorithm that is specially suited to dealing with approximation problems, was introduced in [KMSV94]. Let us start formalizing these concepts.

Let Π be an optimization problem and s and s' be two solutions for the problem considered as boolean vectors. The distance function $\mathcal{D}(s, s')$ is the Hamming distance between s and s'. A δ-**neighborhood** of s, denoted $N(s, \delta)$, is the set of all solutions s' that have distance at most δ from s. A feasible solution s is **locally optimal** if the weight function $V(x, s)$ satisfies

$$\forall s' \in N(s, \delta), \ V(x, s) \geq V(x, s').$$

A δ-**local search algorithm** starts from an initial solution and each iteration moves from the current solution s_i to some solution $s_{i+1} \in N(s, \delta)$ with better cost, until it arrives at a locally optimal solution.

This kind of local search is called **standard local search** or **oblivious local search**. A more generalized method, *non-oblivious local search*, is introduced by Khanna et al. [KMSV94]. The non-oblivious local search was shown to be more powerful than the oblivious one since it permits us to explore in both directions: that of the objective function and that of the distance function.

Definition 9.2.1 *A* **non-oblivious local search algorithm** *is a local search algorithm in which the distance and weight function can be chosen from a class of functions. In particular the weight function is defined to be*

$$\mathcal{F}(e, s) = \sum_{\vec{x}} \sum_{i=1}^{r} p_i \Phi_i(e, s, \vec{x})$$

where r is a constant, Φ_i's are quantifier free first-order formulas and the *profits p_i are real constants. The distance function D is any arbitrary poly-nomial time computable function.*

Khanna et al. [KMSV94] showed that non-oblivious local search provides a good way to approximate MaxSNP problems, showing that every problem in MaxSNP can be approximated within a constant factor by the non-oblivious local search algorithm. However, as we show next, the solution provided by the local search algorithm cannot be approximated within NC unless P = NC. In order to do this we consider a particular case of the Maximum Cut problem presented in Chapter 1.

The Local Maximum Cut problem consists in, given an instance of Maximum Cut and an initial solution s, finding a locally optimum solution, achieved through non-oblivious local search, starting from s.

The Local Maximum Cut problem is non approximable in NC, unless P = NC. We notice here that we do not refer to any method used to approximate the locally optimal solution. This result was obtained in [SX95]. The proof is based on the result from Schaffer and Yannakakis [SY91] showing that Local Maximum Cut (for the case of oblivious local search) is P-complete, and uses a reduction from the Circuit True Gates problem. As we have seen the ϵ–approximation to this problem is P-complete for any $\epsilon \in [0, 1)$

Theorem 9.2.1 *There is an $\epsilon > 0$ such that approximating the Local Maximum Cut problem for any $\epsilon' < \epsilon$ is P-complete.*

The next result shows that if for some optimization problem Π approximate solutions obtained with certain resources cannot be arbitrarily approximated using other resources, then the problem Π itself cannot be approximated in this second setting beyond a certain threshold.

Theorem 9.2.2 *Suppose P $\neq$ NC and let x be any instance of an optimization problem Π. Let $\mathcal{A}$ be an algorithm that approximates Π within ϵ_0 in polynomial time. Then, if the value $\mathcal{A}(x)$ cannot be approximated in NC for $\epsilon < \epsilon_1$, for some $\epsilon_1 \geq \epsilon_0$ then there is a constant $\epsilon_2 \geq \epsilon_1 - \epsilon_0$ such that Π cannot be approximated in NC for $\epsilon < \epsilon_2$.*

Proof Since $\mathcal{A}$ approximates Π within ϵ_0 we have that

$$\frac{1}{1 + \epsilon_0} \leq \frac{\mathcal{A}(x)}{\text{Opt}_\Pi(x)} \leq 1 + \epsilon_0.$$

Suppose that there is an NC algorithm $\mathcal{B}$ that approximates Π within some $\epsilon > 0$, that is

$$\frac{1}{1+\epsilon} \leq \frac{\mathcal{B}(x)}{\mathrm{Opt}_\Pi(x)} \leq 1+\epsilon.$$

Now, we can write

$$\frac{\mathcal{B}(x)}{\mathcal{A}(x)} = \frac{\mathcal{B}(x)}{\mathrm{Opt}_\Pi(x)} \cdot \frac{\mathrm{Opt}_\Pi(x)}{\mathcal{A}(x)}$$

and taking into account that when the problem is a maximization the first ratio is at least 1 and the second is at most 1, and that the reverse relation hold for a minimization problem, we therefore have

$$\frac{1}{1+\epsilon+\epsilon_0} \leq \frac{\mathcal{B}(x)}{\mathcal{A}(x)} \leq 1 + \epsilon\epsilon_0.$$

The last inequality means that we can actually approximate $\mathcal{A}(x)$ within ϵ_1 when $1 + \epsilon + \epsilon_0 \leq 1 + \epsilon_1$ and therefore taking $\epsilon_2 = \epsilon_1 - \epsilon_0$ we get that Π cannot be approximated for any $\epsilon < \epsilon_2$. □

From these results, and using the fact that non-oblivious local search provides an approximation for the Maximum Cut problem, it follows that if $P \neq NC$ there is a constant ϵ such that Maximum Cut cannot be approximated in NC within a factor smaller that ϵ. Moreover, since Maximum Cut is MaxNP-complete under E-reductions and these reductions are approximation preserving, we can conclude that any optimization problem to which Maximum Cut problem can be E-reduced has the same non-approximability property.

Theorem 9.2.3 *If* $P \neq NC$ *then for every problem* Π *that is MaxSNP-hard under E-reductions, there exists a constant ϵ such that Π cannot be approximated in NC for any ϵ' smaller than ϵ.*

The approximation properties of MaxSNP-complete problems under the E-reducibility can be summarized in the following way: Let Π be a MaxSNP-complete optimization problem, there are four constants (not necessarily all distinct) $0 < \epsilon_1 \leq \epsilon_2 \leq \epsilon_3 \leq \epsilon_4$, such that for any constant ϵ the following hold.

- If $\epsilon < \epsilon_1$ then Π cannot be approximated in polynomial time by an ϵ-factor unless $P = NP$ [ALM+92].
- The problem can be approximated in polynomial time for $\epsilon \geq \epsilon_2$ [PY91].

- There is no NC approximation algorithm for Π with approximation factor $\epsilon < \epsilon_3$ unless NC $=$ P [SX95].
- The problem can be approximated in NC for $\epsilon \geq \epsilon_4$ [DST93].

These results relate the accuracy of the approximation with the resources needed to compute it.

Appendix 1

Definition of Problems

In this appendix we give the formal definition of the problems that have been used throughout the survey.

1 **CIRCUIT VALUE**
   Instance: An encoding of a boolean circuit with n gates together with an input assignment.
   Solution: The value of the output gate.

2 **LINEAR PROGRAMMING**
   Instance: An integer $m \times n$ matrix A, an integer m-vector b and an integer n-vector c.
   Solution: A rational n-vector x such that $A x \leq b$.
   Measure: $c^T x$.

3 **HIGH DEGREE SUBGRAPH**
   Instance: A graph $G = (V, E)$.
   Solution: An induced subgraph H of G.
   Measure: The minimum degree of H.

4 **HIGH EDGE CONNECTED SUBGRAPH**
   Instance: A graph $G = (V, E)$.
   Solution: An induced subgraph H of G.
   Measure: The edge connectivity of H.

5 **HIGH LINKAGE SUBGRAPH**
   Instance: A graph $G = (V, E)$.
   Solution: An induced subgraph H of G.
   Measure: The linkage of H, defined as the maximum minimum degree of any of the subgraphs.

6 HIGH VERTEX CONNECTED SUBGRAPH

Instance: A graph $G = (V, E)$.

Solution: An induced subgraph H of G.

Measure: The connectivity of H.

7 LOCAL MAXIMUM CUT

Instance: A graph $G = (V, E)$ together with a partition of V.

Solution: A partition locally optimum for non-oblivious local search.

8 MAXIMUM ACYCLIC SUBGRAPH

Instance: A digraph $G = (V, E)$.

Solution: Subset $E' \subseteq E$ such that $G' = (V, A')$ is acyclic.

Measure: $|E'|$.

9 MAXIMUM 0-1 KNAPSACK

Instance: An integer b and a finite set $I = \{1, \dots, n\}$, for each $i \in I$ an integer size s_i and an integer profit p_i.

Solution: Subset $S \subseteq I$ such that $\sum_{i \in S} s_i \leq b$.

Measure: $\sum_S p_i$.

10 MAXIMUM CLIQUE

Instance: A graph $G = (V, E)$.

Solution: A subset $V' \subseteq V$ such that every two nodes in V' are joined by an edge in E.

Measure: $|V'|$.

11 MAXIMUM CUT

Instance: A graph $G = (V, E)$.

Solution: A subset $V' \subseteq V$ such that no two nodes in V' are joined by an edge in E.

Measure: $|V'|$.

12 MAXIMUM (CARDINALITY) MATCHING

Instance: A graph $G = (V, E)$.

Solution: A subset $E' \subseteq E$ such that each pair of edges in E' has disjoint endpoints.

Measure: $|E'|$.

13 MAXIMUM FLOW

Instance: A network $N = (G, s, t, c)$ where $G = (V, E)$ is a directed graph, s and t are vertices of G and c is a capacity assignment to each edge in the graph.

Solution: A flow pattern, that is an assignment of a non-negative number to each edge of G such that first, there is no edge for which the flow exceeds the capacity and second, for every vertex different from s and t, the sum of the flows in the incoming edges equals the sum of the flows in the outgoing edges.

Measure: The sum of the flows in the incoming edges of t.

14 MAXIMUM INDEPENDENT SET

Instance: A graph $G = (V, E)$.

Solution: A subset $V' \subseteq V$ such that no two nodes in V' are joined by an edge in E.

Measure: $|V'|$.

15 MAXIMUM POSITIVE NOT ALL EQUAL 3SAT (Max Pos NAE 3SAT)

Instance: A set of weighted clauses with at most three literals of the form $NAE(x_1, \cdots, x_3)$ where each x_i is a literal or a constant 0/1, and no clause contains a negated literal. Such a clause is satisfied if its constituents do not all have the same value.

Solution: An assignment to the variables.

Measure: The sum of the weights of the satisfied clauses.

16 MAXIMUM SATISFIABILITY

Instance: A set X of variables, a collection C of disjunctive clauses.

Solution: A subset $C' \subseteq C$ of clauses such that there is a truth assignment for X that satisfies every clause in C'.

Measure: $|C'|$.

17 MAXIMUM G-SATISFIABILITY (B) (MaxGSAT(B))

Instance: A set X of variables, a collection C of conjunctive clauses each with at most B literals.

Solution: A subset $C' \subseteq C$ of clauses such that there is a truth assignment for X that satisfies every clause in C'.

Measure: $|C'|$.

18 MAXIMUM k-SATISFIABILITY (Max$k$SAT)

Instance: A set X of variables, a collection C of disjunctive clauses each with at most k literals ($k \geq 2$).

Solution: A subset $C' \subseteq C$ of clauses such that there is a truth assignment for X that satisfies every clause in C'.

Measure: $|C'|$.

19 MAXIMUM SET PACKING

Instance: A collection C of subsets of a finite set X.

Solution: A subcollection C' of mutually disjoint subsets.

Measure: $|C'|$.

20 MAXIMUM WEIGHT EDGE PACKING

Instance: Given a hypergraph G with vertex weights w.

Solution: An edge packing, that is an assignment p of non-negative weights to the edges of G such that the total weight assigned to the edges adjacent to any vertex v is at most $w(v)$.

Measure: $\sum_{e \in E} p(e)$.

21 MAXIMUM WEIGHT MATCHING

Instance: A graph $G = (V, E)$ with a real weight function w on its edges.

Solution: A subset $E' \subseteq E$ such that each pair of edges in E' has disjoint endpoints.

Measure: $\sum_{e \in E'} w(e)$.

22 MAXIMUM WEIGHT PERFECT MATCHING

Instance: A graph $G = (V, E)$ with a real weight function w on its edges.

Solution: A subset $E' \subseteq E$ such that each pair of edges in E' has disjoint endpoints and every vertex in G is covered.

Measure: $\sum_{e \in E'} w(e)$.

23 METRIC BOTTLENECK TRAVELING SALESPERSON

Instance: A set C of m cities, with a positive integer distance function $(d_{i,j})$ between every two cities satisfying the triangle inequality, an initial city s and a final city f.

Solution: A simple path from s to f passing through all cities.

Measure: The length of the largest distance in the path.

24 MINIMUM BIN PACKING

Instance: A finite set U of items, each $u \in U$ with an integer size $s(u)$, and a positive integer capacity b.

Solution: A partition of U into disjoint $U_1, \ldots, U_m$ such that for every U_i in the partition, $\sum_{u \in U_i} s(u) \leq b$.

Measure: m.

25 MINIMUM k-CENTER

Instance: A complete graph $G = (V, E)$ with integer edge distances d_{ij} satisfying the triangle inequality.

Solution: An $S \subseteq V$ with $|S| = k$.

Measure: $\max_{i \in V} \min_{j \in S} d_{ij}$

26 MINIMUM CUT

Instance: A graph (or digraph) $G = (V, E)$, $|V| = n, |E| = m$, with (or without) edge weights.

Solution: Disjoint partition $S, T \subseteq V$.

Measure: Total number of edges (or its weight) between S and T.

27 MINIMUM (s, t)-CUT

Instance: A graph (or digraph) $G = (V, E)$, $|V| = n, |E| = m$, with (or without) edge weights, and two distinguished vertices s, t.

Solution: Disjoint partition $S, T \subseteq V$ with $s \in S, t \in T$.

Measure: Total number of edges (or its weight) between S and T.

28 MINIMUM k-CUT

Instance: A graph $G = (V, E)$ with non-negative edge weights and k natural.

Solution: A subset $S \subseteq E$ suth that their removal leaves k connected components.

Measure: Total weight of S.

29 MINIMUM DOMINATING SET

Instance: A graph $G = (V, E)$.

Solution: A subset $V' \subseteq V$ such that for each $u \in V - V'$ there is a $v \in V'$ with $(u, v) \in E$.

Measure: $|V'|$.

30 MINIMUM EDGE DOMINATING SET
Instance: A graph $G = (V, E)$.
Solution: A subset $E' \subseteq E$ such that each edge in E shares at least one endpoint with some edge in E'.
Measure: $|E'|$.

31 MINIMUM GRAPH PARTITION
Instance: A graph $G = (V, E)$ and an integer $r \leq |V|$.
Solution: The subset $E' \subseteq E$ that are cut when the nodes of V are partitioned into two sets with sizes $|V|$ and $|V| - r$.
Measure: $|E'|$.

32 MINIMUM JOB SEQUENCING WITH DEADLINES
Instance: A set of n jobs, such that each job i has associated a processing time requirement t_i, a deadline d_i and a profit p_i.
Solution: Find a schedule in one machine.
Measure: The sum of the profits of all jobs that have finished by their deadline times.

33 MINIMUM METRIC TRAVELING SALESPERSON
Instance: A complete graph $G = (C, E)$ representing a set of n cities, with a positive integer distance function $(d_{i,j})$ satisfying the triangle inequality.
Solution: A tour of G.
Measure: $\sum_{(i,j) \in E} d_{i,j}$.

34 MINIMUM MULTIWAY CUT
Instance: A graph $G = (V, E)$, $|V| = n$, $|E| = m$, with (or without) edge weights, and an $S \subset V$.
Solution: A $T \subseteq E$ disconnecting every pair in S.
Measure: Total number of edges (or its weight) in T.

35 MINIMUM m-PROCESSORS SCHEDULING
Instance: A set of n tasks T with an assignment $l(i, j)$ of execution time of task i on processor j.
Solution: An assignment f of tasks to processors.
Measure: $\max_{i \in [1...m]} \sum_{t \in T, f(t) = i} l(t, i)$.

36 MINIMUM m-PROCESSORS SCHEDULING WITH SPEED FACTORS

Instance: A set of n tasks T with an assignment $l(i)$ of execution time of task i, speed factor $s(j) \geq 1$ for each processor j such that $s(1) = 1$.
Solution: An assignment f of tasks to processors.
Measure: $\max_{i \in [1...m]} \sum_{t \in T, f(t)=i} (l(t)/s(i))$.

37 MINIMUM k-SUPPLIER

Instance: A complete bipartite graph $G = (V_1, V_2, E)$ with edge weights $f(e)$ satisfying the triangle inequality.
Solution: A subset $C \subseteq V_2$.
Measure: $\max_{v \in V_1} \min_{c \in C} f(v, c)$.

38 MINIMUM k-SWITCHING NETWORK

Instance: A complete graph $G = (V, E)$ with edge weights $f(e)$ satisfying the triangle inequality.
Solution: A partition $C_1, \ldots, C_{2k}$ of V.
Measure: $\max_{i \in [1...k]} \min_{v_1 \in C_{2i-1}, v_2 \in C_{2i}} f(v_1, v_2)$.

39 MINIMUM TRAVELING SALESPERSON PROBLEM

Instance: A complete graph with edge lengths.
Solution: A tour that covers all the vertices in the graph.
Measure: The tour's total length

40 MINIMUM VERTEX COVER

Instance: A graph $G = (V, E)$.
Solution: A subset $V' \subseteq V$ such that for each $(u, v) \in E$, at least one of u and v belongs to V'
Measure: $|V'|$.

41 MINIMUM SET COVER

Instance: A family of sets C of weighted sets.
Solution: A subfamily $C' \subseteq C$ such that $\bigcup_{S \in fc'} S = \bigcup_{S \in C} S$.
Measure: The total weight of C'.

42 MINIMUM WEIGHT VERTEX COVER

Instance: A graph $G = (V, E)$ and a real weight function w defined on V.
Solution: A subset $V' \subseteq V$ such that for each $(u, v) \in E$, at least one of u and v belongs to V'.
Measure: $\sum_{v \in V'} w(v)$.

43 MULTICOMMODITY FLOW

Instance: A network $N = (G, S, T, c)$ where $G = (V, E)$ is a directed graph, S and T are sets of k sources and k sinks and c is a capacity assignment to each edge in the graph.

Solution: A flow pattern, that is an assignment of k nonnegative numbers to each edge of G such that first, there is no edge for which the flow exceeds the capacity and second, for every vertex not in $S \cup T$ the sum of the flows in the incoming edges equals the sum of the flows in the outgoing edges.

Measure: The sum of the flows in the incoming edges to T.

44 PERFECT MATCHING

Instance: A graph $G = (V, E)$ with $|V| = 2n$.

Solution: A subset $E' \subseteq E$ such that each pair of edges in E' has disjoint endpoints, with $|E'| = n$.

45 POSITIVE LINEAR PROGRAMMING

Instance: An integer $m \times n$ matrix A, an integer m-vector b and an integer n-vector c, such that all coefficients involved are positive.

Solution: A rational n-vector x such that $A x \leq b$.

Measure: $c^T x$.

46 SHORTEST COMMON SUPERSTRING

Instance: A finite alphabet Σ, a finite set L of strings from Σ^*.

Solution: A string $w \in \Sigma^*$ such that every $x \in L$ is a substring of w.

Measure: $|w|$.

47 SUBSET SUM

Instance: An integer b and a finite set $I = \{1, \ldots, n\}$, for each $i \in I$ an integer size s_i.

Solution: Subset $S \subseteq I$ such that $\sum_{i \in S} s_i \leq b$.

Measure: $\sum_S s_i$.

48 CIRCUIT TRUE GATES NUMBER

Instance: An encoding of a boolean circuit of n gates together with an input assignment.

Solution: The number of gates that output **true**.

Measure: $c^T x$

Bibliography

[ACC90] R. Alverson, D. Callahan, and D. Cummings. The TERA computer system. In *Supercomputing 90*, pages 1–6. IEEE Computer Society Press, 1990.

[ACC+95] A. Andreev, A. Clementi, P. Crescenzi, E. Dahlhaus, S. de Agostino, and J. Rolim. The parallel complexity of approximating the high degree subgraph problem. In *6th ISAAC*, volume 1004 of *Lecture Notes in Computer Science*, pages 145–156. Springer-Verlag, Berlin, 1995.

[ACG+96] G. Ausiello, P. Crescenzi, G. Gambosi, V. Kann, and A. Marchetti-Spaccamela. Approximate solution of hard combinatorial optimization problems. With a compendium of NP optimization problems. Technical report, Universita degli Studi di Roma, La Sapienza, 1996.

[ACP96] G. Ausiello, P. Crescenzi, and M. Protasi. Approximate solution of NP optimization problems. *Theoretical Computer Science*, 96:1–48, 1996.

[ADK+93] F. Abolhassan, R. Drefenstedt, J. Keller, W. Paul, and D. Scheerer. On the physical design of PRAMs. *The Computer Journal*, 36:733–744, 1993.

[ADKP89] K. Abrahamson, N. Dadoun, D. Kirkpatrick, and K. Przytycka. A simple parallel tree contraction algorithm. *Journal of Algorithms*, 10:287–302, 1989.

[ADP80] G. Ausiello, P. D'Atri, and M. Protasi. Structure preserving reductions among convex optimization problems. *Journal of Computer and System Sciences*, 21:136–153, 1980.

[Akl89] S.G. Akl. *The Design and Analysis of Parallel Algorithms*. Prentice-Hall, New York, 1989.

[AL93] B. Awerbuch and T. Leighton. A simple local-control approximation algorithm for multicommodity flow. In *34th IEEE Symposium on Foundations of Computer Theory*, pages 459–468. IEEE Computer Society Press, 1993.

[ALM+92] S.R. Arora, C. Lund, R Motwani, M. Sudan, and M. Szegedy. Proof verification and hardness of approximation problems. In *33rd IEEE Symposium on Foundations of Computer Science*, pages 14–23. IEEE Computer Society Press, 1992.

[AM86] R.J. Anderson and E.W. Mayr. Approximating P-complete problems. Technical report, Stanford University, 1986.

[AMW89] R.J. Anderson, E.W. Mayr, and M.K. Warmuth. Parallel approximation algorithms for Bin Packing. *Information and Computation*, 82:262–277, 1989.

[ASE92] N. Alon, J.H. Spencer, and P. Erdös. *The probabilistic method.* Wiley-Interscience, New York, 1992.

[Bak83] B. Baker. Approximation algorithms for NP-complete problems on planar graphs. In *24th IEEE Symposium on Foundations of Computer Science*, pages 265–273. IEEE Computer Society Press, 1983.

[Bak85] B. Baker. A new proof for the first-fit decreasing Bin Packing algorithm. *Journal of Algorithms*, 6:49–70, 1985.

[Bak94] B. Baker. Approximation algorithms for NP-complete problems on planar graphs. *Journal of the ACM*, 41:153–180, 1994.

[BDG88] J.L. Balcazar, J. Díaz, and K. Gabarró. *Structural Complexity I.* Springer-Verlag, Heidelberg, 1988.

[Bel96] M. Bellare. Proof checking and approximation: Towards tight results. *SIGACT News*, 27:2–13, 1996.

[Ber90] B. Berger. *Using randomness to design efficient deterministic algorithms.* PhD thesis, Department of Electrical Engineering and Computing Science, Massachusetts Institute of Technology, 1990.

[BGJR88] F. Barahona, M. Grötschel, M. Jünger, and G. Reinelt. An application of combinatorial optimization to statistical physics and circuit layout design. *Operation Research*, 36:493–513, 1988.

[BJL+91] A. Blum, T. Jiang, M. Li, J. Tromp, and M. Yannakakis. Linear approximation of shortest superstrings. In *23th ACM Symposium on the Theory of Computing*, pages 328–336. ACM Press, 1991.

[BL76] K. Booth and G. Lueker. Testing for the consecutive ones property, interval graphs and graph planarity using PQ-algorithms. *Journal of Computer and System Sciences*, 13:335–379, 1976.

[Bre73] R.P. Brent. The parallel evaluation of general arithmetic expressions. *Journal of the ACM*, 21:201–208, 1973.

[BRS89] B. Berger, J. Rompel, and P. Shor. Efficient NC algorithms for set covering with applications to learning and geometry. In *30th IEEE Symposium on Foundations of Computer Science*, pages 54–59. IEEE Computer Society Press, 1989.

[BS90] B. Berger and P. Shor. Approximation algorithms for the maximum acyclic subgraph problem. In *1st SIAM–ACM Symposium on Discrete Algorithms*, pages 236–243. ACM Press, 1990.

[Chr76] N. Christofides. Worst-case analysis of a new heuristic for the travelling salesman problem. Technical report, Graduate School of Industrial Administration, Carnegie-Mellon University, 1976.

[Chv79] V. Chvátal. *Linear Programming.* Freeman, San Francisco, 1979.

[CK95] P. Crescenzi and V. Kann. A compendium of NP optimization problems. Technical report, Universita degli Studi di Roma, La Sapienza, 1995.

[CKP+93] D. Culler, R.M. Karp, D. Patterson, A. Sahay, K.E. Schauser, E. Santos, T. Subramonian, and T. von Eicken. Logp: Towards a realistic model of parallel computation. In *ACM SIGPLAN Symposium on Principles and Practice of Parallel Programming*, pages 478–491. ACM Press, 1993.

[CKST95] P. Crescenzi, V. Kann, R. Silvestri, and L. Trevisan. Structure in approximation classes. In *Computing and Combinatorics Conference*, volume 959 of *Lecture Notes in Computer Science*, pages 539–548. Springer-Verlag, Berlin, 1995.

[CLR89] T. H. Cormen, Ch. Leiserson, and R. Rivest. *Introduction to Algorithms*. The MIT Press, Cambridge, Mass., 1989.

[CN89] M. Chrobak and J. Naor. An efficient parallel algorithm for computing large independent sets in a planar graph. In *1st ACM Symposium on Parallel Algorithms and Architectures*, pages 379–387. ACM Press, 1989.

[CNS82] N. Chiba, T. Nishizeki, and N. Saito. An approximation algorithm for the maximum independent set problem on planar graphs. *SIAM Journal of Computing*, 2:663–675, 1982.

[Coh92] E. Cohen. Approximate max flow on small depth networks. In *33rd IEEE Symposium on Foundations of Computer Science*, pages 648–658. IEEE Computer Society Press, 1992.

[Coo71] S. Cook. The complexity of theorem-proving procedures. In *3rd ACM Symposium on the Theory of Computing*, pages 151–158. ACM Press, 1971.

[Coo81] S.A. Cook. Towards a complexity theory of synchronous parallel computation. *L'Enseignement Mathematique*, 27:94–124, 1981.

[DFF56] G.B. Dantzing, L. Ford, and D. Fulkerson. A primal–dual algorithm for linear programs. In H.. Kuhn and A.W. Tucker, editors, *Linear Inequalities and Related Systems*, pages 171–181. Princeton University Press, 1956.

[DJP+92] E. Dahlhaus, D.S. Johnson, C. Papadimitriu, P.D. Seymour, and M. Yannakakis. The complexity of multiway cuts. In *24th. ACM Symposium on the Theory of Computing*, pages 241–251. ACM Press, 1992.

[DST93] J. Díaz, M.J. Serna, and J. Torán. Parallel approximation schemes for planar graphs problems. In T. Lengauer, editor, *1st European Symposium on Algorithms*, volume 726 of *Lecture Notes in Computer Science*, pages 145–156. Springer-Verlag, Berlin, 1993.

[DST96] J. Díaz, M.J. Serna, and J. Torán. Parallel approximation schemes for problems on planar graphs. *Acta Informatica*, 33:387–408, 1996.

[Eve79] S. Even. *Graph Algorithms*. Computer Science Press, Potomac, Md, 1979.

[Fag75] R. Fagin. Monadic generalized spectra. *Zeitschrift für Mathematische Logik und Grundlagen der Mathematik*, 21:123–134, 1975.

[FdlVL81] W. Fernandez de la Vega and G.S. Lueker. Bin packing can be solved within $1 + \epsilon$ in linear time. *Combinatorica*, 1:349–355, 1981.

[FF62] L.R. Ford and D.R. Fulkerson. *Flows in Networks*. Princeton University Press, 1962.

[FW78] S. Fortune and J. Wyllie. Parallelism in random access machines. In *10th ACM Symposium on Theory of Computation*, pages 114–118. ACM Press, 1978.

[GH88] O. Goldschmidt and D. Hochbaum. Polynomial algorithm for the k-cut problem. In *29th IEEE Symposium on Foundations of Computer Sciences*, pages 444–451. IEEE Computer Society Press, 1988.

[GHR95] R. Greenlaw, H.J. Hoover, and W.L. Ruzzo. *Limits to parallel computation: P-completeness theory*. Oxford University Press, 1995.

[GJ79] M.R. Garey and D.S. Johnson. *Computers and Intractability: A Guide to the Theory of NP-Completeness*. Freeman, San Francisco, 1979.

[GJS76] M.R. Garey, D.S. Johnson, and L. Stockmeyer. Some simplified NP-complete graph problems. *Theoretical Computer Science*, 1:237–267, 1976.

[GL78] G.V. Gens and E.V. Levner. Approximate algorithms for certain universal problems in scheduling theory. *Izv. Akad. Nauk SSSR, Tekh. Kibernet.*, 16:38–43, 1978.

[Gol78] L.M. Goldschlager. A unified approach to models of synchronous parallel machines. In *10th ACM Symposium on Theory of Computing*, pages 89–94. ACM Press, 1978.

[GR88] A. Gibbons and W. Rytter. *Efficient Parallel Algorithms*. Cambridge University Press, 1988.

[Gra66] R.L. Graham. Bounds for certain multiprocessing anomalies. *Bell Systems Technical Journal*, 45:1563–1581, 1966.

[GRK91] P.S. Gopalakrishnan, I.V. Ramakrishnan, and L.N. Kanal. Approximate algorithms for the Knapsack problem on parallel computers. *Information and Computation*, 91:155–171, 1991.

[GS93] A. Gibbons and P. Spirakis, editors. *Lectures on Parallel Computation*. Cambridge University Press, 1993.

[GSS82] L.M. Goldschlager, R.A. Shaw, and J. Staples. The maximum flow problem is log-space complete for P. *Theoretical Computer Science*, 21:105–111, 1982.

[GVY96] N. Garg, V. Vazirani, and M. Yannakakis. Approximate max flow min (multi)cut theorems and their applications. *SIAM Journal of Computing*, 25:235–251, 1996.

[GW96] M. Goemans and D. Williamson. The primal–dual method for approximation algorithms and its application to network design problems. In D.S. Hochbaum, editor, *Approximation Algorithms for NP-hard problems*, pages 83–138. PWS Publishing Company, Boston, Ma, 1996.

[Har67] F. Harary. Problem 16. In M. Fiedler, editor, *Graph Theory and Computing*, page 161. Czech. Academy Sciences, Prague, 1967.

[Has96] J. Håstad. Clique is hard to approximate within $n^{1-\epsilon}$. In *37th IEEE Symposium on Foundations of Computer Sciences*, pages 627–636. IEEE Computer Society Press, 1996.

[HCS79] D.S. Hirschberg, A.K. Chandra, and D.V. Sarwate. Computing connected components on parallel computers. *Communications of the ACM*, 22:461–464, 1979.

[Hoc82] D.S. Hochbaum. Approximation algorithms for the set cover and the vertex cover. *SIAM Journal of Computing*, 11:555–556, 1982.

[Hoc96] D.S. Hochbaum, editor. *Approximation Algorithms for NP-hard problems*. PWS Publishing Company, Boston, Ma, 1996.

[HS76] E. Horowitz and S.K. Shani. Exact and approximate algorithms for scheduling nonidentical processors. *Journal of the ACM*, 23:317–327, 1976.

[HS86] D.S. Hochbaum and D.B. Shmoys. A unified approach to approximation algorithms for bottleneck problems. *Journal of the ACM*, 33(3):532–550, 1986.

[HS87] D.S. Hochbaum and D.B. Shmoys. A best possible parallel approximation algorithm to a graph theoretic problem. *Operational Research*, pages 933–938, 1987.

[IK75] O. Ibarra and C.E. Kim. Fast approximation algorithms for the knapsack and sum of subsets problem. *Journal of the ACM*, 22:463–468, 1975.

[JaJ92] J. JáJá. *An introduction to parallel algorithms*. Addison-Wesley, Reading, Mass., 1992.

[JDU+74] D.S. Johnson, A. Demers, J. Ullman, M. Garey, and R. Graham. Worst case performance bounds for simple one-dimensional bin packing algorithms. *SIAM Journal on Computing*, 3:299–326, 1974.

[Joh74] D.S. Johnson. Approximation algorithms for combinatorial problems. *Journal of Computer and System Sciences*, 9:256–278, 1974.

[JPY88] D.S. Johnson, C. Papadimitriu, and M. Yannakakis. How easy is local search? *Journal of Computer and System Sciences*, 37:79–100, 1988.

[JS82] J. JáJá and J. Simon. Parallel algorithms in graph theory: Planarity testing. *SIAM Journal on Computing*, 11:313–328, 1982.

[JV87] D.B. Johnson and S.M. Venkatesan. Parallel algorithms for minimum cuts and maximum flows in planar networks. *Journal of the ACM*, 34:950–967, 1987.

[Kan92] V. Kann. *On the approximability of NP-complete optimization problems*. PhD thesis, Department of Numerical Analysis and Computing Science, Royal Institute of Technology, Stockholm, 1992.

[Kar72] R.M. Karp. Reducibility among combinatorial problems. In R.E. Miller and J.W. Thatcher, editors, *Complexity of Computer Computations*, pages 85–104. Plenum Press, NY, 1972.

[Kar86] H.J. Karloff. A las Vegas RNC algorithm for maximum matching. *Combinatorica*, 6:387–392, 1986.

[Kar93] D.R. Karger. Global min-cuts in RNC and other ramifications of a simple min-cut algorithm. In *4th SIAM-ACM Symposium on Discrete Algorithms*, pages 757–765. ACM Press, 1993.

[KK82] N. Karmarkar and R.M. Karp. An efficient approximation scheme for the one-dimensional bin packing problem. In *23rd IEEE Symposium on Foundations of Computer Science*, pages 312–320. IEEE Computer Society Press, 1982.

[KLS89] G.A. Kindervater, J.L. Lenstra, and D.B. Shmoys. The parallel complexity of TSP heuristics. *Journal of Algorithms*, 10:249–270, 1989.

[KM94] D.R. Karger and R. Motwani. Derandomization through approximation: An NC algorithm for minimum cuts. In *26th ACM Symposium on the Theory of Computing*, pages 497–506. ACM Press, 1994.

[KMSV94] S. Khanna, R. Motwani, M. Sudan, and U. Vazirani. On syntactic versus computational views of approximability. In *35th IEEE Symposium on Foundations of Computer Science*, pages 2–10. IEEE Computer Society Press, 1994.

[KR86] P.H. Klein and J.H. Reif. An efficient parallel algorithm for planarity. In *27th IEEE Symposium on Foundations of Computer Science*, pages 465–477. IEEE Computer Society Press, 1986.

[KR90] R.M. Karp and V. Ramachandran. Parallel algorithms for shared memory machines. In Jan van Leewen, editor, *Handbook of Theoretical Computer Science, Vol. A*, pages 869–942. Elsevier Science Publishers, Amsterdam, 1990.

[KS80] B. Korte and R. Schrader. On the existence of fast approximation schemes. *Nonlinear Programming*, 4:415–437, 1980.

[KS88] L. Kirousis and P. Spirakis. Probabilistic log-space reductions and problems probabilistically hard for P. In R. Karlsson and A. Lingas, editors, *1st Scandinavian Workshop on Algorithm Theory*, volume 318 of *Lecture Notes in Computer Science*, pages 163–175. Springer-Verlag, Berlin, 1988.

[KSS93] L.M. Kirousis, M.J. Serna, and P. Spirakis. The parallel complexity of the connected subgraph problem. *SIAM Journal on Computing*, 22:573–586, 1993.

[KT96] L.M. Kirousis and D.M. Thilikos. The linkage of a graph. *SIAM Journal on Computing*, 25:626–647, 1996.

[KUW86] R.M. Karp, E. Upfal, and A. Wigderson. Constructing a perfect matching is in Random NC. *Combinatorica*, 6:35–48, 1986.

[KVY93] S. Khuller, U. Vishkin, and N.A. Young. Primal–dual parallel approximation technique applied to weighted set and vertex cover. In *3rd IPCO Conference*, pages 333–341, 1993.

[Lad75] R.E. Ladner. The circuit value problem is log space complete for P. *SIGACT News*, 7:18–20, 1975.

[Law76] E.L. Lawler. *Combinatorial Optimization: Networks and Matroids*. Holt, Rinehart and Winston, NY, 1976.

[Lei93] F.T. Leighton. *Introduction to Parallel Algorithms and Architectures: Arrays, Trees, Hypercubes*. Morgan Kaufmann, Calif., San Mateo, CA., 1993.

[Lev73] L. Levin. Universal sequential search problems. *Problems of Information Transmissions*, 9:265–266, 1973.

[LMR86] G. S. Lueker, N. Megiddo, and V. Ramachandran. Linear programming with two variables per inequality in poly-log time. In *18th ACM Symposium on Theory of Computing*, pages 196–205. ACM Press, 1986.

[LN93] M. Luby and N. Nisan. A parallel approximation algorithm for positive linear pogramming. In *25th ACM Symposium on Theory of Computing*, pages 448–457. ACM Press, 1993.

[LP86] L. Lovasz and M.D. Plummer. *Matching Theory*. North-Holland, Amsterdam, 1986.

[LT79] R.J. Lipton and R.E. Tarjan. A separator theorem for planar graphs. *SIAM Journal on Applied Mathematics*, 36:177–189, 1979.

[LT80] R.J. Lipton and R.E. Tarjan. Applications of a planar separator theorem. *SIAM Journal on Computing*, 9:615–627, 1980.

[Lub86] M. Luby. Removing randomness in parallel computation without a processor penalty. In *29th IEEE Symposium on Foundations of Computer Science*, pages 162–173. IEEE Computer Society Press, 1986.

[McC93] W.F. McColl. General purpose parallel computers. In A. Gibbons and P. Spirakis, editors, *Lectures on Parallel computation*, pages 337–391. Cambridge University Press, 1993.

[ML37] S. Mac Lane. A structural characterization of planar combinatorial graphs. *Duke Mathematical Journal*, 3, 1937.

[Mot92] R. Motwani. Lecture notes on approximation algorithms – volume I. Technical report, Stanford University, 1992.

[MR86] G.L. Miller and V. Ramachandran. *Efficient parallel ear decomposition with applications*. Technical report MSRI, Calif., Berkeley, 1986.

[MR95] R. Motwani and P. Raghavan. *Randomized Algorithms*. Cambridge University Press, 1995.

[MVV87] K. Mulmuley, U. Vazirani, and V. Vazirani. Matching is as easy as matrix inversion. In *19th ACM Symposium on Theory on Computing*, pages 355–365. ACM Press, 1987.

[NC88] T. Nishizeki and N. Chiba. *Planar graphs: theory and algorithms*. North-Holland, Amsterdam, 1988.

[NI92] H. Nagamochi and T. Ibaraki. Computing edge connectivity in multigraphs and capacitated graphs. *SIAM Journal of Discrete Mathematics*, 5(1):54–66, 1992.

[Ofm63] Y. Ofman. On the algorithmic complexity of discrete functions. *Soviet Physics–Doklady*, 2(4):589–591, 1963.

[Pap94] C. Papadimitriou. *Computational Complexity*. Addison-Wesley, Reading, Mass., 1994.

[Pip79] N. Pippenger. On simultaneous resource bounds. In *20th IEEE Symposium on Foundations of Computer Science*, pages 307–311. IEEE Computer Society Press, 1979.

[PR87] J.G. Peters and L. Rudolph. Parallel aproximation schemes for subset sum and knapsack problems. *Acta Informatica*, 24:417–432, 1987.

[PS82] C. Papadimitriou and K. Steiglitz. *Combinatorial Optimizations, Algorithms and Complexity*. Prentice-Hall, Englewood Cliffs, NJ, 1982.

[PY91] C. Papadimitriou and M. Yannakakis. Optimization, approximation, and complexity classes. *Journal of Computer and System Sciences*, 43:425–440, 1991.

[PY93] C. Papadimitriou and M. Yannakakis. The travelling salesman problem with distances one and two. *Mathematics of Operations Research*, 18:1–11, 1993.

[Rag88] P. Raghavan. Probabilistic construction of deterministic algorithms: approximating packing integer programs. *Journal of Computer and System Sciences*, 37:130–143, 1988.

[Ran96] A. Ranade. Bandwidth efficient parallel computation. In F. Meyer auf der Heide and B. Monien, editors, *23rd International Colloquium on Automata, Language and Programming*, Lecture Notes in Computer Science, pages 4–23. Springer-Verlag, Berlin, 1996.

[Rei93] J. Reif. *Synthesis of Parallel Algorithms*. Morgan Kaufmann, New York, 1993.

[RHG93] S. Ravindran, N.W. Holloway, and A. Gibbons. Approximating minimum weight perfect matchings for complete graphs satisfying the triangle inequality, with a logarithmic performance ratio is in NC. In *19th International Workshop on Graph Theoretic Concepts in Computer Science (WG'93)*, volume 790 of *Lecture Notes in Computer Science*, pages 11–20. Springer-Verlag, Berlin, 1993.

[RR89] V. Ramachandran and J. Reif. An optimal parallel algorithm for graph planarity. In *34th IEEE Symposium on Foundations of Computer Science*, pages 282–287. IEEE Computer Society Press, 1989.

[RV89] S. Rajagopalan and V. Vazirani. Primal–dual RNC approximation algorithms for the (multi)-set (multi)-cover and covering integer programs. In *34th IEEE Symposium on Foundations of Computer Science*, pages 322–331. IEEE Computer Society Press, 1989.

[Sch80] J.T. Schwartz. Fast probabilistic algorithms for verifications of polynomial identities. *Journal of the ACM*, 27:701–717, 1980.

[Ser90] M.J. Serna. *The parallel approximability of P-complete problems*. PhD thesis, Department LSI, Universitat Politècnica de Catalunya, 1990.

[Ser91] M.J. Serna. Approximating linear programming is log-space complete for P. *Information Processing Letters*, 37:233–236, 1991.

[Sha75] S. Shani. Approximate algorithms for the 0/1 knapsack problem. *Journal of the ACM*, 22:115–124, 1975.

[Spi93] P. Spirakis. PRAM models and fundamental parallel algorithm techniques: Part II. In A. Gibbons and P. Spirakis, editors, *Lectures on Parallel Computation*, pages 41–66. Cambrige University Press, 1993.

[SS89] M.J. Serna and P. Spirakis. The approximability of problems complete for P. In H. Djidjev, editor, *Proceedings in Optimal Algorithms*, volume 401 of *Lecture Notes in Computer Science*, pages 193–204. Springer-Verlag, Berlin, 1989.

[SS91] M.J. Serna and P. Spirakis. Tight RNC approximations to Max Flow. In *8th Symposium on Theoretical Aspects of Computer Science*, volume 480 of *Lecture Notes in Computer Science*, pages 118–126. Springer-Verlag, Berlin, 1991.

[SV91] H. Saran and V. Vazirani. Finding k-cuts within twice the optimal. In *32th IEEE Symposium on Foundations of Computer Science*, pages 743–751. IEEE Computer Society Press, 1991.

[SX95] M.J. Serna and F. Xhafa. On parallel versus sequential approximation. In P. Spirakis, editor, *3rd European Symposium on Algorithms*, volume 979 of *Lecture Notes in Computer Science*, pages 145–156. Springer-Verlag, Berlin, 1995.

[SY91] A.A. Schaffer and M. Yannakakis. Simple local search problems that are hard to solve. *SIAM Journal of Computing*, 20:56–87, 1991.

[Tut47] W.T. Tutte. The factorization of linear graphs. *Proceedings of the London Mathematical Society*, 22:107–111, 1947.

[Tut63] W.T. Tutte. How to draw a graph. *Proceedings of the London Mathematical Society*, 3(13), 1963.

[TY93] S. Teng and F. Yao. Approximating shortest superstrings. In *34th IEEE Symposium on Foundations of Computer Science*, pages 158–165. IEEE Computer Society Press, 1993.

[Val90] L.G. Valiant. A bridging model for parallel computation. *Communications of the ACM*, 33:103–111, 1990.

Author index

Subject index